In Bolivia

In Bolivia

Eric Lawlor

Vintage Books A Division of Random House, Inc. New York

VINTAGE DEPARTURES

A Vintage Departures Original, November 1989

First Edition

Copyright © 1989 by Eric Lawlor

All rights reserved under International and Pan-American Copyright Conventions. Published in the United States by Random House, Inc., New York, and simultaneously in Canada by Random House of Canada Limited, Toronto.

Library of Congress Cataloging-in-Publication Data
Lawlor, Eric.
  In Bolivia / by Eric Lawlor.—1st ed.
  p.   cm.—(Vintage departures)
  ISBN 0-394-75836-6: $7.95 (pbk.)
  1. Bolivia—Description and travel—1981–   I. Title.
F3315.L38   1989
984—dc19   88-40387
                                                      CIP

Book design by Chris Welch

Manufactured in the United States of America
10 9 8 7 6 5 4 3 2 1

For Christopher Lawlor
(1917–1986)

Preface

I F I T weren't for indecision, Bolivia wouldn't exist at all. Simón Bolívar, for whom the country is named, initially opposed its independence. His vision of a single republic embracing all of South America didn't admit of Bolivian autonomy. But the rivalry between Peru and Argentina had to be considered. Unless he did something to contain it, his grand design didn't stand a chance. So what would Bolivia be? Part of a continental confederation or a buffer state?

Bolívar dithered and dithered—and finally washed his hands of the matter. It was left to his general, Antonio Sucre, to determine Bolivia's fate. Sucre opted for independence, a decision that the British vice-consul in Lima promptly denounced as setting an evil precedent and boding ill for the country's peace and security.

The equivocation surrounding its origins in 1825 may explain why there has always been something paradoxical about Bolivia's existence. The country developed slowly—and with qualified results. Even today there are those who challenge its right to call itself a nation. With much of the national territory still to be secured, Bolivia, they say, is a nation only in name.

What surprises is that Bolivia exists at all. Many of its leaders have seemed intent on destroying it. In 1843 a British diplomat described life in the young republic as "a series of perfidious revolutions and usurpations of power, shameless robberies of the public treasury, extortions of tribute from the indigenous Indians and constant wars without a military object."

There followed a century of attrition. Ruled by regimes either indifferent to its interests or incapable of defending them, Bolivia saw its national territory shrink as all five of its neighbors gained ground at its expense. The country today is half the size it was at independence. Yet for some, Bolivia, even as presently constituted, is still too big. The country's more extreme detractors advocate dissolving it altogether. Since there is no compelling reason why it should exist, they say, Bolivia should be apportioned among Brazil, Argentina, and Peru.

Although Korea has been called the hermit nation, the sobriquet describes Bolivia at least as well. Locked in the center of the South American continent, Bolivia was left to its own devices. Bypassed by travelers, it was forgotten to the extent that in 1904 the Bolivian chargé d'affaires in London was asked to settle an argument: Would he say exactly where Bolivia was? In Bohemia or South Africa? Writing ten years later, Paul Walle complained that "if there is one country amongst all others concerning which our knowledge is scanty, and even at fault, it is this one."

Nearly half a century later, Bolivia was still terra incognita. "There is no other country in the world which contributes so little to the general stock of information," Harold Osborne wrote in 1954. "Even in South America, there are few who wish to know more of it than fanciful and slightly malicious gossip."

In 1970 André Malraux described Bolivia as "one of the

few morally unexplored civilized regions in the world." (He might also have said *physically* unexplored, since parts of it still awaited the cartographer.) And in 1981 Robert Alexander, a leading Bolivianist, commented that "the average U.S. citizen is very ignorant of Bolivia. . . . The average [cocaine] dealer in any U.S. city may know more about [it] than do the majority of his compatriots."

Until recently Bolivia was one of the most inaccessible countries in the world. Bordered on the west by the Andes and on the north and east by the Amazon jungle, it deterred all but the most determined. Even today many travelers avoid it. Unlike Montaigne, who boasted that he liked discomfort, few anymore prize hardship.

Yet difficult as travel in Bolivia is, it was once more so. Today one can make the trip from La Paz to Santa Cruz in twenty-four hours. Sixty years ago it could have taken as long as twelve months—the precise journey time depending on the availability of mule trains. With few exceptions *paceños* stayed in La Paz, *cruceños* in Santa Cruz. Foreigners showed themselves no less reticent. The urge of Ishmael was not so fierce that Bolivia couldn't be resisted. The country was secluded, off the beaten track, and it featured on few itineraries. It didn't even boast a "European" capital. La Paz, until twenty years ago, was fairly primitive, and those coming here were warned to expect few of the comforts of civilization.

Bolivia is more remarkable for those who might have come—and didn't. Rudyard Kipling, for example. In 1927 Kipling spent five weeks in Brazil, long enough to visit Bolivia, had he wanted. But it can't have called. Or if it did he wasn't listening. Charles Darwin also visited Brazil. Bolivia can't have called him either. Nor did it call Richard Burton, although he spent four years in Santos in the 1860s. Four boring years. The Byronic Burton was desperate for adventure. Bolivia would certainly have provided it. Even the intrepid

Teddy Roosevelt, "determined to cross the Andes," bypassed Bolivia for Argentina and Chile, taking as his route "the easiest and most accessible" of the southern passes.

R. B. Cunninghame Graham, the Scot who spent much of his life in South America and wrote some fifty stories and essays about it, was another who stayed away. Variously described as the last of the conquistadors and a modern Don Quixote, Cunninghame Graham corresponded with Oscar Wilde, provided Joseph Conrad with material for *Nostromo*, and inspired George Bernard Shaw's *Captain Brassbound's Conversion*. He once said that he longed to be far from "the unnecessary, necessities of life." Bolivia, at the time, was as far as one was likely to get.

Left to itself Bolivia became, in Robert Alexander's words, "one of the most agitated and most picturesque nations in South America." Yet "agitated" is inadequate to describe its politics. Since independence in 1825, Bolivia has had sixteen constitutions and nearly 250 governments, each lasting an average of ten months. At times it boasted several governments, while at others it had none at all. In 1849 the American ambassador had to wait three months before an administration materialized to which he could present himself.

Much of this instability was the fault of the nineteenth-century caudillos, the most notorious of whom was Mariano Melgarejo. Max Daireaux, the French writer, described him as "the grandiose man, extravagant and fatal, who pushes to the extreme the virtues and vices of his time: bravery and cruelty, ignorance and vanity, audacity, arrogance, contempt for death, contempt for men, a kind of burlesque and sanguinary demi-god, a monstrous aberration of the genius of history."

The reality was less lyrical. Dubbed the *caudillo bárbaro*, Melgarejo mortgaged Bolivia to foreign banks and made deals that would eventually cost the country its Pacific seaboard. Bolivia has never reconciled itself to the loss of its coast. A century later regaining a port on the Pacific remains its top foreign-policy objective.

The caudillos had an intellectual heir in Daniel Salamanca, who in 1932 declared war on neighboring Paraguay when it seized a fort in the Chaco. Actually the fort belonged to Paraguay and had been seized by Bolivia six weeks earlier in a years-old border dispute. It didn't matter. Salamanca, besieged by problems at home, had his diversion. Bolivia was to lose this war—South America's biggest and most bitter armed conflict. In all, some 90,000 people died. Two-thirds of them were Bolivians.

It was largely as a consequence of the Chaco War that in 1952 this volatile little country experienced one of the continent's most dramatic revolutions. In just two years land was redistributed, the tin mines appropriated, and the army neutralized. In this century Latin America has seen only two other revolutions like it—Mexico's in 1910 and Cuba's, which would not occur for another seven years.

Despite the revolution Bolivia's upper class remains virtually intact. The families who ruled this country at independence dominate its affairs to this day. History provides few more startling examples of tenacity. Yet it was precisely this that Che Guevara meant to challenge when he chose Bolivia as the country from which to launch his continental revolution in 1966. Guevara and his small band of insurgents were quickly destroyed. Bolivia, which has resisted most efforts to change it, had defeated one of guerrilla warfare's greatest theoreticians.

Bolivia endures. But even today its future is as much an open question as ever. After Haiti it is the poorest country in Latin America. Yet living standards continue to fall, and there is little chance of any turnaround. As the government struggles to bring the economy back from ruin, its efforts are being opposed by powerful elements within Bolivia itself. In a society in which Western and indigenous traditions seem incapable of merging, those with money to invest would rather send it overseas.

A further threat is posed by the cocaine barons, whose financial resources now exceed those of the central government. (One of them, Roberto Suárez, once offered to repay Bolivia's entire foreign debt.) The *cocaleros* own several major banks and have helped elect some of Bolivia's most prominent politicians. Their power is extensive—as they demonstrated in 1980 by installing the cocaine regime of General Luis García Meza.

Bolivia must also contend with Brazilian efforts to bring it within that country's sphere of influence. Since its involvement in the coup that overthrew President Juan José Torres in 1971, Brazil has established a "pole of development" in the Bolivian department of Santa Cruz, an area rich in oil and natural gas. Illegal immigration into the region and the presence of Brazilian investors have sparked fears that Brasília may be fostering secessionist sentiment.

But more than the economy, or the *cocaleros*, or Brazil, it is the Indians finally who will determine what happens in Bolivia. Although they constitute 70 percent of the population and may now vote, many live a marginal existence. This is something few recent governments have done anything to change. But until the Indians are integrated, Bolivia's future will remain uncertain. To guarantee its survival, Bolivia must become a society that commands the loyalty of all its citizens.

In Bolivia

1

M Y F I R S T lunch in La Paz would have been unremarkable but for the earthquake. I had just begun to eat when the table started to shake. Knowing little about Bolivian cuisine, my instinct was to blame the *plato típico* I had ordered—a quantity of fat, it turned out. Then my water glass crashed to the floor. It was joined there, a moment later, by the saltcellar. A second glass fell, and then a third—these from the next table. It too was shaking.

A woman screamed, and a man shouted something unintelligible. The chandelier began to jingle. I glanced out the window. The buildings across the street appeared to ripple. It was as if they were underwater. And then the shaking stopped.

"Surely that can't be what I think it is," I said to the man at the next table. "I thought Bolivia didn't have earthquakes."

"It's an earthquake all right," he said. Fright had made him the color of lemon peel. He fumbled in his pockets. "Do you have a cigarette?" he asked.

Before I could answer a low rumbling filled the room, and the shaking resumed. This time there was widespread panic. With much shrieking people tried to conceal themselves beneath their tables. Several made a dash for the street. A child wailed. The waiter glanced at the ceiling. The chandelier was now describing a wide arc. Then the rumbling ceased, and it was quiet again.

"Is it finished?" a woman whispered. She was crouched behind a chair. Her companion knelt beside her, his hands covering his head. "Let's hope so," he said without looking up.

The man who wanted a cigarette now asked for a match.

"I'm sorry you had to experience that," he said, as if the earthquake were his responsibility.

"I'm just a bit perplexed," I said. "I'd read that Bolivia didn't suffer earthquakes. One of your ambassadors to Washington said so. Surely he wouldn't lie? Not to the National Geographic Society?"

"Bolivia suffers everything," said the man. "It is our tragedy that we are immune to nothing."

I ventured out in some trepidation, but La Paz appeared to be intact, its shabbiness unscathed. What character this city has derives from its location and its population. For the rest, it is unprepossessing. It doesn't surprise then that no grand conception attended its founding in 1548.

In many of South America's Indian cultures, a city's shape alluded to the structure of the universe. The founders of La Paz lacked the temperament for cosmic symbolism. Their city did not seek to model itself on the constellations nor did it try to copy some divine model. La Paz was to be a mere settlement, established where it was, and allowed to assume what shape it would, because gold had been found nearby. It was to be what St. Augustine would have called a terrestrial place. Thus was its character established from the start.

Besides being the highest capital in the world, La Paz is also the most precipitous. More than 12,000 feet above sea level, it fills the floor and walls of a narrow canyon. This

accounts for its unique geography. There are but two direc-
tions here: up and down, with up predominating. If in Los
Angeles there is no "there" there, in La Paz "there" is invariably at the top of a 10 percent gradient. An earthquake
that levels this city will confer an inestimable benefit on the
tourist industry.

Had G. K. Chesterton come here, La Paz might have cured
him of his love of hills. Chesterton prized Brighton for its
steepness. All those "sudden ascents and disappearances, of
mazes and openings into eternity" made him feel he was in
an Albrecht Dürer print. There are none of Dürer's clean-
cut stereometric solids in La Paz, no prisms, cubes, cylinders,
and obelisks clustering like crystals. The work of Dürer's this
city put me most in mind of is the representation of hell in
Allerhailsamste Warnung.

It is easy to recognize those who are new here: They are
blue in the face and either thrust unnaturally forward as they
labor uphill or thrust unnaturally back as they inch their way
down. It is hard to say which is more perilous. Going up,
your heart pounds and your lungs scorch. Up, up, you slog,
fighting panic and the urge to collapse in a doorway. Then,
as the air thins, your vision blurs. But this is as well. It's
better not to see that cruel slope hovering above you like
Jacob's ladder.

Coming down inspires a different kind of terror. Now the
enemy is gravity. But much as you fight it, it won't be resisted.
You realize to your horror that you've broken into a run, that
you are gathering speed. Your momentum builds until you
can no longer control yourself. Down, down you go, ever
faster. At the sight of you, people leap into doorways. Mothers
pluck their babies from your path. And then you're airborne.
The cobblestones have done it again. Polished by the years
to a high sheen, they provide as much traction as a ski run.

It is tempting to stay in one's hotel room. And one probably would, if it were remotely comfortable. But many of the hotels in La Paz are rudimentary. Here are some selections pulled randomly from *The South American Handbook*—the Austria: "can be unpleasant due to drug dealing"; the Yanacocha: "has seen better days"; the Italia: "can be very noisy"; the Vienna: "dubious"; Residencial Chuquisaca: "best avoided."

So you venture out and, because La Paz lacks more conventional attractions, go in search of the lamppost from which President Gualberto Villaroel was hanged in 1946. In Plaza Murillo, it is directly across the street from the Presidential Palace. A sobering sight for incumbent presidents, it may explain why so many Bolivian communities are still without streetlights.

In a country with hardly a proletariat to speak of, Villaroel enjoys the curious status of proletarian hero. His death place has become a minor shrine. A small monument marks the spot: a bust—the neck is massive—and below it a tablet recording two of the president's aphorisms. Neither suggests a talent for demagogy: "A captain doesn't abandon his ship during a storm"—had Villaroel forgotten that Bolivia is landlocked?—and "I am not an enemy of the rich, but I am a friend of the poor."

If this latter statement was intended to reassure the one while placating the other, it didn't work. Convinced that the president meant them no good, the oligarchy mustered a mob and stormed the Presidential Palace. That, at any rate, is the legend. Actually the Villaroel regime was one of the most violent and repressive ever to rule Bolivia. Its practice of jailing and killing those opposed to it alienated much of the population. The people who hanged Villaroel on July 14, 1946—Bastille Day—were disaffected members of the middle class.

Villaroel was not the first Bolivian head of state to meet an untimely end. The list of presidents and former presidents to die violently is extensive. Pedro Blanco was assassinated in 1829; Sucre in 1830; Jorge Córdova in 1861; Belzú in 1866; Melgarejo in 1871; Agustín Morales in 1872; Hilarión Daza in 1894; and José Manuel Pando in 1917. Nor did the tradition end in 1946. President René Barrientos died in a highly suspicious helicopter crash in 1969, and former President Torres was gunned down in Buenos Aires in 1972. Becoming chief of state in this country often amounts to signing one's death warrant.

Villaroel is one of the few republican figures commemorated in La Paz. This is largely a consequence of Bolivia's fractious politics. One faction's hero is another faction's tyrant. But some of the blame also attaches to Bolivian historiography. When the past is revised as often as it is here, statuary has the potential to be very embarrassing.

It doesn't surprise then that so many monuments honor abstractions: the Unknown Soldier, or Bolivia herself—a figure suspiciously like Athena. An uncompromising foot on the neck of an enemy, she extends an olive branch with one hand while clutching fast a formidable sword with the other. This, it should be remembered, is a country that hasn't won a war in its history.

I got to Plaza Murillo in time to see the new German ambassador arrive at the presidential palace. The Colorados—the president's praetorian guard—were drawn up in his honor. Their uniforms are nineteenth century—white trousers, red jackets, white gloves, and plumed hats. But their trousers were not very white, their jackets less than red, and their hats didn't plume nearly enough. The effect was rather shabby. Much as you might see in an amateur production of Donizetti's *Daughter of the Regiment*.

While I waited for the ambassador to emerge after presenting his credentials, I fell into conversation with one of Bolivia's bureaucrats. Bernardo by name, he was mainly concerned about the upcoming World Cup quarterfinal pitting Argentina and England. "It will be a massacre," he said sadly.

Several times during the course of our conversation, he relocated us. "Those people are plainclothes policemen," he said, nodding in the direction of four huddled men. "They have tape recorders." Our conversation was not in the least compromising—unless one included his complaint that the evenings in La Paz were sometimes chilly. Did he really think them interested in our chat about the World Cup?

"You don't know them," he said. "But let's not talk about them. You haven't told me what brought you to Bolivia."

No accident. *Bolivia* was the first word I ever spoke. As legend has it, I was being fed an egg one morning when I swept my plate to the floor and bellowed "Bolivia" at the top of my voice. From my mother's reaction, it might be supposed that I had uttered an imprecation. To a woman who stressed the value of custom, shouting geographic names at the breakfast table was a breach of all the established rules. She spent the rest of the day "lying down."

My father, more phlegmatic, took it better—although it's possible he was thinking and didn't hear me. He did a lot of thinking—with the result that he rarely noticed us. It was said by way of excuse that he felt the world's problems "keenly." And such was my respect for him that for years afterward I aspired to being keen too. I imagined it the mark of high seriousness.

Bolivia doesn't often figure in the infant vocabulary, and my outburst might have been singular but for two things. One was my age. I was three at the time, and, far from being smart, I was considered rather slow. At six I had still to learn to read. (It is true that at six Lina Waterfield couldn't read either. But that changed when Matthew Arnold threatened to jail her parents. I didn't know Matthew Arnold and paid dearly for it. I was an adolescent before I could read with any ease.)

Another consideration is that my birth, in 1951, was eclipsed, at least for my parents, by the revolution that swept Bolivia twelve months later. For the next three years that event excluded all else from their consideration. It was all they talked about.

Bolivia became a particular obsession with my father. An obsession, I should explain, in a series of obsessions. As a consequence of his feeling keenly about the world, there were few trouble spots that failed to absorb his interest. In 1949 he didn't notice when his business failed. India, recently independent, had his attention. In 1951 his business partner committed suicide. But again his mind was elsewhere: Korea was making news. And by the time, a year later, he was embezzled of what little money he had left, there was Bolivia to occupy him. After all, what was money when a country 6,000 miles away was in the throes of remaking itself?

It became vital to my father that Bolivia's revolution succeed, and events in that small country were weighed as if the future of the race depended on them. Our breakfast table became a war room; the morning papers were scrutinized as if they were dispatches from the front. What elation when the new government nationalized the tin mines! My mother fetched a jar of her best plum jam. A week later peasants protesting food prices rioted in La Paz. A bad sign this, and my father declined a second egg. The next day the news was even worse—the government had declared a state of siege— and to dramatize the gravity he attached to this development, my father refused breakfast altogether. Instead he took a turn around the garden. I found him there an hour later, humming as he pruned his roses. How brave, I remember thinking. Had I any Latin, no doubt the remark of St. Benedict would have occurred to me: *Ecce labora et noli contristari*—"There he works and refuses to be gloomy."

Things soon looked up though. The Americans resumed aid to the new regime, and my parents danced around the kitchen. To see them, you'd have thought it was *they* who were to get the money. Not even the news the next day that the Bolivian cabinet had resigned could dampen their spirits.

Then, in 1956, the government introduced what it called "a stabilization program," and the revolution was over. It didn't matter. My father had long ago lost interest. Other crises called. Ivan's tanks rolled through Budapest, and Nasser had claimed the Suez Canal as his own.

For my part, an affection for Bolivia had been established, and afterward I was to take a more than passing interest in what happened there. The news was never very cheering. Bolivia resisted reform. Nothing lasted long: governments, presidents, constitutions, even architecture—disgruntled citizens had twice put the presidential palace to the torch.

The country's politics were silly even by the standards of the region. Yet as well as being comic, its turbulence was almost admirable. Order battled chaos—and always got the worst of it. Bolivia seemed ungovernable, and I cheered its unruliness. It was a place where reason deferred to impetuosity. And why shouldn't it? What is decorum, after all, but a kind of tyranny? Like Rousseau's natural man, I found more to prize in stormy freedom than in tranquil subjection.

"How long do you think you'll be here?" asked Bernardo.

"Oh, several months, I should think."

"Well, don't be surprised if, at the end of it, you've had your fill of stormy freedom." He pointed to the building behind him. "Have you visited the cathedral?"

"Should I?"

"It's something of a curiosity. Construction began shortly

after independence. As you can see, it's still not finished. They're still working on two of the cupolas."

Why the delay?

He rubbed together thumb and forefinger. "No money."

When they were building the exterior walls, he explained, workers would lay a tier of stones and bank the sides with earth. This created two inclined planes, along which the next tier of stones could be rolled into position. But there was a problem when the walls were finished. Since the earth inside the cathedral could only be removed through the doors and windows, it took thirteen years to clear the place.

By confiscating its property in the 1820s, Sucre broke the economic power of the church in Bolivia. Even so, this action hardly explains such massive dilatoriness. A century and a half is a long time. The Egyptians, after all, built the Great Pyramid in twenty years, as long as it took Shah Jahan to build the Taj Mahal. The Parthenon was built in nine years and the Church of Santa Sophia in only five.

"We complete nothing in this country," said Bernardo. "Even our revolution was abandoned. We dislike conclusions. In our hearts, we expect things to turn out badly. And why not? Doesn't our history confirm it?"

He looked so distressed, I felt compelled to console him. "Oh, a hundred and fifty years isn't all that long. Bear in mind that it took three centuries to build Reims Cathedral."

"True, but they had to deal with the Hundred Years' War and the Free Companies."

"Well, Siena never completed *its* cathedral. They never got further than the baptistry."

"Why?"

I was hoping he wouldn't ask. "I think the Black Death had something to do with it."

He looked distressed again. "We deserve an unfinished

cathedral," he said, sighing. "It's emblematic. After all, we are an unfinished country. Bolivia is all process. There is the appearance of activity, but nothing ever happens. All that effort, and nothing to show for it. All the activity cancels out."

He glanced anxiously at the secret police, one of whom chose just then to look in our direction. We had to relocate again.

The ambassador emerged, finally, and a brass band played—first Bolivia's anthem, and then West Germany's. I would have expected protocol to require a reversal of that order. Fortunately, offense, if any was intended, was not taken, and the ambassador, after bowing low to the Colorados, was driven away to a hot lunch. I hoped, for his sake, that it wouldn't be a *plato típico*.

Troops with machine guns surrounded the palace. Surely the presentation of credentials by the ambassador of a friendly country didn't warrant such precautions?

"The government claims that people are plotting to assassinate the president," said Bernardo.

"Is that likely?"

He shrugged. "Who knows? In the absence of real dangers, we invent imaginary ones. We are long past the stage of being able to tell one from the other."

The soldiers stood around casually when I watched them from the center of the plaza. But when I moved closer for a better look, they became suddenly serious, fixing me with their full attention and clenching their guns very tight. I quickened my pace, pausing at the corner to glance back. I was still being watched. After that I avoided Plaza Murillo as much as I could.

Soldiers stood guard all over the city. Since many of them seemed to be protecting nothing more significant than tailor shops, the intention can only have been to keep them busy.

All in all, they seemed to enjoy themselves. Jostling one another like schoolboys, they killed time by grinning at passing
girls. Their military service might better have been called
military flirting.

I walked back to my hotel and telephoned a man named
Héctor. He and I have a mutual friend in London. She had
given me a letter of introduction, which I was to take to him.
"He is very well-to-do and very well connected," she had said,
giving me to believe that he was the flower of his generation.
"If you want to know what's happening in Bolivia, Héctor is
the one to tell you."

"Come by this evening," he said when I called. "I'll send
a car at eight."

He wasn't home when I arrived. "He had to go out," said
Carmen, one of the maids. "But he won't be long. He wants
you to look around the house until he gets back."

This surprised me because the house was really rather
awful. The furniture, the carpets, the draperies—everything
in it was uniformly dreadful and can only have been chosen
to cause offense. I have been in homes in which Georgian
mirrors, Victorian sideboards, and Chippendale wing chairs
vied with Gothic chests, Sheraton cabinets, and Carolean
love seats. But this was no inspired hodgepodge. I was reminded of a provincial museum whose curator's budget exceeded his discrimination.

I entered the sitting room through an arch papered with
simulated lapis lazuli. I reared back in alarm. The walls were
covered by a blue-and-red flocked silk. An imitation Meissen
jar stood by the fireplace. The mantelpiece and tables were
swathed in green damask banded with pink and yellow. The
room was a riot of cabriole legs. A badly carved ivory table
from India, an aging leather couch, an unattractive Empire
clock, a Regency bureau—a poor copy—filled with cheap
trinkets. . . . It took the breath away.

The entrance to the dining room was marked by two bronze does and an umbrella stand filled with cannonballs. The room's most striking feature was the trompe l'oeil back wall—a pair of illusory columns led into a colonnade stretching as far as a small gazebo. The curtains were trimmed with several tones of red fringe, and the wallpaper—Gothic revival—was heavily patterned with floral reliefs in purple and blue.

On a table in the hall were souvenirs from Atlantic City, Niagara Falls, and Miami, places one would hesitate to visit, let alone advertise having been there. There was a brutish innocence about the place. Suddenly I dreaded meeting Héctor.

But I wouldn't have to. Not that evening anyway. Carmen entered with a message: Héctor had called to say that his business detained him. Might we meet some other evening? Tomorrow, perhaps?

Perhaps.

I didn't expect to hear from him again, but he surprised me by turning up at my hotel the next morning.

"I am going to take you to the Valley of the Moon," he said.

"That's very kind of you, but I had planned to go to Tiahuanaco."

"Why would you want to go there?" he wanted to know.

"As I understand it, it has some of the finest ruins on the continent."

"Those Indian civilizations are vastly overrated. The Valley of the Moon is much more interesting. Come!"

I could visit Tiahuanaco another time. Héctor was a mover and shaker in this society, and there was much I wanted to ask him.

But to my disappointment, he seemed disinclined to talk about Bolivia.

Did he think Congress would approve the new tax code?

"You never know," he said.

"The government says the president's life is in danger."

"Is he ill?"

"No. It claims that someone is trying to kill him. You hadn't heard?"

"It's news to me."

We lapsed into silence.

Then Héctor spoke. "Who do you think is the better shot—Prince Charles or Prince Philip?"

He had been educated in England, and the experience had made him a confirmed Anglophile. His absorbing interest was the royal family.

Did I like Dick Francis? he wanted to know.

"I don't believe I've ever read him."

"Never? He's the queen mother's favorite writer. The queen mother once invited a friend of mine to spend the night at Sandringham. And what was on his night table? A Dick Francis novel!"

Did his friend enjoy Sandringham?

"Oh, yes. Though he caught rather a bad cold. His room was heated by one of those electric fires. The sort with several bars? One of the bars didn't work."

He had a subscription to *The Tatler* and went to London once a year to have his shirts made. Now thirty-seven, he had returned to Bolivia when his father died, four years earlier.

"Someone had to take over the business. My sister wasn't interested. She lives in New York. That left only me."

"What kind of business is it?"

"We own several office buildings."

"You survived the revolution then?"

"A storm in a teacup. We lost some land, but most of our money was in London."

He claimed to miss England terribly. "What fun I used to

have. All those drinks parties in Knightsbridge. We'd get smashed and then drive into the country and change all the road signs."

But even more than the "drinks parties," he missed the porridge.

"Porridge? But I saw oatmeal on sale in the market just this morning."

"Yes, but it's not the same, is it?"

"Maybe not."

The Valley of the Moon, Héctor explained, is named for its lunar appearance. The formations are the result of wind and rain erosion. The shapes are very striking. Rising to a height of 30 or 40 feet, they are of a gray clay that crumbles when you touch it. They look like something Dubuffet might have done, although they have none of his sense of play. Indeed, they are just a bit unnerving. The columns appear truncated. They seem to stop at the neck. Where are their heads? And the absence of color makes them even more anonymous. It is as if they had rid themselves of distinguishing marks. What are they concealing?

I had the feeling suddenly that I was failing to understand something. Vital information was being withheld. I thought of Héctor and his reticence in the car. Why would he have been so evasive when I mentioned the tax code? And surely someone like him had to have known about the government's conspiracy claims. Unless . . . Heavens, no! Surely Héctor wasn't one of the conspirators?

The silence was shattered by gunfire.

My heart somersaulted. "What in God's name was that?" I asked.

"Nothing to worry about," he said, laughing. "There's a skeet club up the road. Let's go back to the house for a drink."

I didn't want to see that house again. Nor, if he was planning to assassinate anyone, did I want to see Héctor.

"That seems like an awful lot of trouble."

"No trouble at all. Come!"

Back at the house, Carmen was dispatched to make a flask of pisco sours. She was new here and very tentative. She walked on tiptoe, terrified that she would upset something. As recently as two weeks ago, Héctor told me, Carmen had worn traditional Indian costume. What diminution! She now sported a blue shop coat and coarsely seamed nylon stockings. The stockings were much too big for her: the excess gathered in deep folds around her ankles. And, crime of crimes, she had cut her marvelous Indian hair. Whatever would have made her do it?

"Money," said Héctor. "Like a drink?"

"That's quite a step for her, abandoning one culture for another. Do you think she's done the right thing?"

"Well, she can hardly stay an Indian all her life," he said a little crossly.

"No?"

"The Indians are premodern. Why do you think Bolivia is backward?"

He was astonished when I suggested that Carmen was attractive. "Attractive?" he said. "You mean you would consider sleeping with an Indian?"

"Why not?"

"Because they're repulsive. Now let's talk about something sensible. I want to give a garden party. Do you know how to make scones?"

"You combine butter, flour, eggs, and sugar, I think. But in what proportions, I've no idea. Perhaps someone at the British embassy can tell you."

"Oh, I never talk to them. There's not an old Etonian among them. Another drink?"

The pisco sour had made me bold. "If I may be frank," I said, "you seem a bit reactionary. I got the impression this morning that you wouldn't mind at all if the president *were* killed."

"Me? I'm apolitical. I don't much care what happens in Bolivia. Most of my friends are in England. If *I* may be frank, I can't understand why you'd want to come here."

"I hope to prove my father wrong. He imagines Bolivia a kind of Hobbesian hell. But then he's a man who values the steady symmetries."

The steady symmetries, rational inquiry, proportion. Especially proportion. My father saw the elements constituting a whole only as long as they did what was expected of them. He admired the Greeks, despised excess, and, like the Stoics, regarded the emotions as disturbances of the soul.

My father and I were antitheses. He enjoyed the Haydn symphonies, and I found them vapid. I liked my gardens rank and gross and gone to seed. His was designed along lines laid down for such things by the architects of Versailles. His pear trees, horribly misshapen, grew on espaliers and never failed to remind me of the Inquisition. Although if he hoped to extract a confession from them, he didn't succeed. As far as I know, they never recanted. His great interest for a time was topiary. Three of our yew trees were mutilated by him until they bore a vague resemblance to a horse, a camel, and an elephant. But the effect can't have pleased him. Shortly afterward he had the trees cut down. He replaced them with a greenhouse.

If he could have, my father would have rearranged the stars. The natural made him so uncomfortable that he would joke about it. It was his "party piece" when there were guests in the house. What is unforgivable about nature, he would begin, is the sheer quantity of it. "To say it's everywhere is not to exaggerate. What an appalling waste of space." Yet he did not propose eliminating it altogether. It had, on occasion, served us well, and for this reason, if for no other, parts of it deserve to be preserved—if only to convince future generations that they were missing nothing.

"People who speak of returning to nature are atavists and no punishment is too harsh for them," he said. "As for communing with nature, what might one say to it? More to the point, what might it possibly have to say to one? No, nature is a devouring monster and an unwholesome bully, and something should be done about it. We have acquiesced long enough."

He despised the Romantics. Coleridge especially. It was Coleridge who had said, "In nature, there is nothing melancholy." This was hard to understand, said my father, because even Coleridge must have noticed that in England it rains all the time. "He can't have known what he was talking about. Or perhaps, like most of the English pastoralists, he eulogized the great outdoors from the comfort of his London club."

Augustinian by temperament, my father took a stern view of his fellows. To his mind being virtuous entailed being rational, and since men eschewed reason, they would always be mischief makers. Remove the threat of sanctions and they would devour one another. He claimed to see the rational structure behind appearances, and not all the books in Don Quixote's library would have shaken this belief. There was no mystery, only ignorance. But men would always be ignorant, and this was why they needed a strong state. That was Bolivia's problem, he said. There was no law in the place. Which was why the revolution had so interested him. It had tried to change that, and it had failed. Bolivia was living in a state of nature—not the Golden Age described by Rousseau but the state of barbarism imagined by Hobbes.

Remember Hobbes? he would ask. "There is no place for industry because the fruit thereof is uncertain . . . no navigation . . . no commodious buildings . . . no account of time;

no arts; no letters; no society; and, which is worst of all, continual fear and danger of violent death; and the life of man, solitary, poor, nasty, brutish and short." Didn't that describe Bolivia rather well?

Did it? I wasn't sure. It is certainly true that Bolivian society affords the individual a degree of freedom with few modern parallels. I was curious to know how this freedom had developed. Why had authority in Bolivia failed to make its will effective? Why make personal liberty the paramount value? And what happens to civic virtue if you do? I wanted to know too what freedom in such quantity had wrought. Does living in Bolivia place one at the mercy of individual whim? Or is this country proof that people don't need regulation? Maybe there is something to prize in all this ferment. Has Bolivia perhaps stumbled on a better way to reconcile right and interest? Might it not represent an existence more civilized than my own?

To answer these questions, I would have to learn something about Bolivia's past. (Bolívar and Melgarejo seemed especially interesting.) And then I would have to meet its current actors: the miners and the Indians, the drug traffickers and the army, the middle class and survivors of the Chaco War. Each had had a major impact on this country. Remove any one of them, and Bolivia would not be the place it is today.

Héctor laughed. "Are you in for a surprise! You should have listened to your father."

"I don't believe you like this country."

"Of course I don't like it. It's a dump. All of South America is a dump."

"Brazil isn't a dump."

"Have you ever been there?"

"Well, no."

"Then believe me: it's a dump."

"You aren't going to tell me that Argentina is a dump."

"You've been to Argentina?"

"Not yet."

"Stay away from it. It's another dump."

"And Peru?"

"The biggest dump of all."

I'd begun to find this man rather tiresome.

"I really must be going," I said. "I've got a busy day tomorrow."

"Doing what?"

He'd caught me on the hop. "I thought I'd . . . visit a tin mine." It was the first thing that came to mind. But I was glad it had. It would be my chance to meet some miners.

"Which tin mine?"

"Siglo Veinte. The biggest tin mine in the world."

"What an odd person you are!" He looked genuinely baffled. Then his expression cleared. "But they'll never let you."

"Who won't?"

"COMIBOL—the mining commission. You can't visit the mines without a letter of authorization. They'll never give you one."

"Well, I can ask."

At COMIBOL the next morning the receptionist directed me to the Tourism Department. Tourism sent me to Public Relations, where I found myself addressing a woman wearing a coat and gloves. The building wasn't heated, and it was bitterly cold.

She explained that the person who issued letters of authorization was out of the country. "Can you wait?" she wanted to know.

"You expect him back sometime soon?"

"A week, two weeks. . . . It's hard to say."

"I can't wait that long, I'm afraid. Isn't there anyone else who can give me a letter?"

"Why do you want to visit the mines?" she said blowing on her hands.

I could hardly tell her I was avoiding Héctor.

"I'm curious as to what they're like."

"Curious?" she repeated. Clearly this wasn't reason enough. I began to extemporize.

"Well, I'm aware of the great importance of mining in Bolivia, the historical role of tin, the political significance of the miners . . ." I ground to a halt.

"Yes?"

". . . and . . . and I'm interested in the working conditions. I've been in the mines in northern England, and I should like to see how they compare."

"Do you know Arthur Scargill?" she asked.

"Not personally, no."

"I think you need the Tourism Department. Tell them exactly what you've told me. They'll give you a letter."

Back in Tourism, I was directed to a seat. An hour elapsed, and then I was shown into a small office. The occupant was a man in his fifties. He seemed genuinely pleased to see me. Perhaps he was bored. His desk had nothing on it. Knowing a little of Bolivia's values by now, I told him how flattered—and grateful—I was that he would make the time to see me.

"So you want to visit the mines," he said. "I don't see that presenting any problem. When did you plan to go?"

"Oh, not anytime soon. Next week, the week after. . . . I really haven't decided."

This was a mistake.

"Oh," he said, "then there's no urgency. Why don't you, in that case, come back and see me next week. Say Thursday. At three o'clock?"

"It isn't possible to get a letter today?"

"Next week would be better."

"If right now isn't convenient, I'd be happy to come back this afternoon."

"Until Thursday then." He guided me toward the door.

"The letter needn't be long. A couple of lines, no more."

"Good-bye."

The experience left me perplexed, and I mentioned it that afternoon to Bernardo, the civil servant I'd met in Plaza Murillo. We had arranged to have tea in a *confitería*.

"It was within his power to write that letter," I said. "A simple thing. He could have done it right then and there. So why wouldn't he?"

Bernardo looked amused. "Certainly, it was within his power. But what kind of power is that? Puny! You express your gratitude, and he never sees you again. So what does he do? He tells you that you must wait a week, you must come back, you must apply to him a second time for this letter. His power is not so puny now, is it? That is the way power is used in Bolivia: to impede, to obstruct. You will get your letter next week. When he has had his fun."

And Bernardo was right. I did.

As I left the *confitería* after tea, a man raced past at such speed that I had to jump out of his way to avoid a collision. This was unusual. People rarely ran in this city. The altitude didn't encourage it. But this man defied convention for good reason. He was being chased.

His pursuer was a respectable bourgeois who, despite being elderly, was remarkably quick on his feet. Nor was anything the matter with his lungs. "Thief, thief," he bellowed. "My wallet. Thief."

The pickpocket darted across the street and made it around the next corner. But the aggrieved bourgeois was closing on him. By now, too, his shouts had drawn some notice, and the chase was joined by two policemen, furiously blowing whistles, and several members of the unemployed, glad of the diversion.

I feared for the pickpocket's safety. I remembered *Arabia Deserta* and Charles Doughty protesting the punishment of the caravan thief: "It was perilous for me to tempt so many strangers' eyes, but as humanity required, I called to them, Sirs; this man may not bear more, hold or he may die under your handling." If I could help it, this pickpocket would not be harmed.

I was not as fast as the others, and when I came level with them, a man was lying on the pavement. I could see little of him. A policeman was sitting on his chest, and another lay across his legs. It was not until they pulled him to his feet that I saw him clearly. There had been a mistake. This was not the man who had nearly knocked me over. That man had been wearing a brown sweater. This one wore a red jacket. I could hardly think that in the heat of the chase he'd had either time or opportunity to change his clothes.

"You have the wrong person," I told one of the policemen.

He glanced at his colleague. My intervention was not appreciated.

"You saw the crime?" he asked.

"Well, no—"

"The stolen wallet was yours?"

"No, but—"

"In that case, please don't interfere."

I looked around for the aggrieved bourgeois, but the crowd had now grown considerably, and I couldn't find him. If I wasn't to be arrested myself, there seemed little I could do. And then I remembered Héctor. Héctor had connections. I'd call him.

But he wasn't terribly interested.

"The police know what they're doing," he said when I telephoned. "I wouldn't get involved if I were you. But I'm glad you called. Come over to the house. There's something I want to show you."

He was admiring a picture over the mantelpiece when Carmen showed me into the drawing room.

"It's a Sisley landscape."

"I don't remember seeing that before. Is it new?"

"Yes. I've just taken delivery of it," he said. "Sisley is my favorite painter. He was English, you know."

"Well, of English descent. Is there nothing you can do for that man? The one they arrested?"

"Best to stay out of it. His father exported artificial flowers to South America."

"Whose father?"

"Sisley's."

"Is that why you like him?"

"No. I admire his loyalty. All the other Impressionists, you know, went on to something else. Sisley stuck with Impressionism till he died."

I was beginning to understand why he would appreciate such dogged adherence. Héctor believed in history. As well he might, of course. History obviously believed in him. But he had convinced himself that his being born into a well-to-do, upper-class family was no accident. History might be inscrutable, but it had its reasons. As it had had its reasons for making him who *he* was, it had had its reasons for making the Indians who *they* were. Even that case of mistaken identity this afternoon—history again. Mysterious, unfathomable history. What could a person do but accept it? However arbitrary it seemed, you embraced your fate.

"Do you like Sisley?" Héctor asked.

"Not terribly. I think he can't have liked people very much. They appear in his pictures very rarely. He never painted his wife and only once painted his children. His villages are always deserted. It's almost as if people didn't exist for him."

Héctor laughed. "I wouldn't blame him for that. People can be an awful bore."

I'd had enough of Héctor. He was an aristocrat without the aristocrat's sense of duty. He had wealth and status and power, yet it mattered not to him that the society he presided over was slowly disintegrating. He produced nothing and provided no leadership. He was not very smart, had few skills, and, as for being decent, his contempt for his countrymen and his belief in his own superiority were not typical of what is normally considered moral.

Morality aside, one is entitled to demand of wealth that those who enjoy it create, at least for themselves, an imaginative way of living. Héctor had failed to do even that. His money had benefited no one—least of all himself. Wealth was wasted on him. He made me ponder, once again, the utility of letters of introduction.

"You'll want to meet the right people," said the woman in London who knew him. By which she meant members of the upper class. But such people are almost never right for one's purposes. In South America the upper classes pride themselves on their loyalty to the ancestral ways. European ways. In their care one is taken to the races, Italian restaurants, concerts of German music, receptions at the Alliance Française. The indigenous is scrupulously avoided.

There is really no substitute for making one's own way in a place. Which is why, in the Latin countries, I recommend the plaza. There, the elderly congregate. Although age may have deprived these people of their vigor, in its place it has given them sobriety. If you would know why a country is the way it is, these are the men to tell you.

But let them befriend you. These are circumspect fellows, and they value propriety. So sit quietly. If you interest them, you will become aware of their glances. Now is the time to look around. You appear surprised to see them. You hadn't realized you had company. You nod and smile. The nod and smile are returned.

They will begin by inquiring about your nationality. "Are you German? English?" (They will never ask if you are American. To do so is considered rude.) Your itinerary is the next order of business, and then you will be asked if you like Bolivia. When you wax on its many virtues, any misgivings they may have about you quickly evaporate. You have been accepted.

Ask one of them if you might see his newspaper. "Of course," he will say. You glance at the front page, appear to consider its import, and then offer some general comment. The vaguer the better. It would be a mistake at this stage to reveal an ideological bent. You are here, after all, to hear *their* views; it isn't necessary that they hear yours. And then you wait.

Expect to wait some time. These men are by no means rash. Although lesser minds might respond immediately to your remark that Congress is still debating the tax bill, these fellows will want to weigh its implications. "And they'll be debating it till Judgment Day," one of them may say eventually. The others will nod gravely. "Why on earth?" you will ask. And then and there they will lay bare the intricacies of national politics.

In La Paz I had one of these seers inquire as to who was the president of England.

"England doesn't have a president," I explained. "The queen is the head of state, of course, but the chief executive is the prime minister, Mrs. Thatcher."

"What kind of man is this Thatcher?" was his next question.

"Mrs. Thatcher"—I was careful to emphasize the *Mrs.*—"is authoritarian. She"—and I stressed the *she*—"doesn't listen to counsel. There is concern that her"—I paused significantly after *her*—"policies will inflict long-term social damage."

The seer nodded wisely. "Just the sort of man we need in Bolivia," he said. "This country needs a strong hand."

While you talk, expect to be hounded by the shoeshine boys. They make one regret having shoes at all. Indeed on one occasion they proved so persistent that I was forced, finally, to remove my footwear altogether and carry it wrapped in my jacket.

Many of them claim to sell tiny artifacts from the ruins at Tiahuanaco. "Original," they hiss conspiratorially. One is expected to believe that they sell these things at great personal risk, although the items in question have every appearance of being mass produced. "No, no," you tell them. But still they importune. "I tell you I don't want it." And finally they go away. Thank God, you think. But a moment later they're back again, hawking the same spurious wares. Perhaps they imagine that you've had a change of heart, that they would only just have turned their backs when you'd think, My God, I must be crazy! Here I am, offered a piece of crude junk for a mere thirty dollars, and I go and pass it up. I could kick myself.

It was to escape the assiduities of one of these people that I stepped into a restaurant one afternoon to eat a second lunch. The waiter recommended the *plato típico*.

"What does it comprise?" I asked.

"That depends."

"On what?"

"What day it is."

"Today, if I am not mistaken, is Saturday. What does it comprise on Saturdays?"

"Normally, it's chicken."

"Normally?"

"Yes. Today, we don't have any."

"Ah! You're telling me there *is* no *plato típico*."

"Oh, yes! There is always a *plato típico*."

"What, then, is it?"

"I don't know. But it's usually very good. You'll enjoy it."

"Very well, then. Let me have it. Whatever it is."

The man at the next table was very drunk. He sat sprawled in his chair with his head thrown back. He was sound asleep.

"Is he all right?" I asked the waiter.

"He's upset because Brazil lost to France in the World Cup," he said. "I've telephoned his wife. She's coming down to take him home."

The man's wife duly arrived and, in the way the women will here, began to coax and cajole him, rubbing the back of his neck. Awake now, he became truculent, forcing away her hand and demanding to be left alone. He began to berate her, becoming steadily more abusive. And then I heard him say, "I'm going to kill you."

I could hardly believe my ears. I glanced over to see if he might possibly mean it—and the man was staring at me. It was I he was threatening to kill.

He got to his feet with great difficulty and began to weave in place. His wife grabbed his waist to steady him.

He glared in my direction. "Imperialist," he said. "What have you ever done for my country except exploit it? Well, you won't exploit it anymore."

He began to struggle out of his jacket.

"Please sit down," said his wife.

"Shut up," he said wittily. With both fists raised, he now started unsteadily toward me. "Get to your feet," he said. "Fight like a man."

He got nearer and nearer. Finally he was standing over me.

"I won't tell you again," he said. "Get up."

But the effort of speaking proved too much for him. His

eyes went suddenly blank, his body sagged, and he pitched forward across my table. He was asleep again. I'm afraid my *plato típico* ruined his shirt.

He was not the only one upset by Brazil's defeat. All of La Paz had taken it to heart, and nearly everyone was drunk. One man, stumbling across the street, collapsed onto the hood of a waiting taxi. He too had fallen asleep. This was a shame because, had he managed to stay awake just a minute longer, he would have seen something most unusual: a man taking a stroll while pulling behind him a dead dog.

The dog had been killed by a car, and the man had tied a rope around its neck. The body bounced over the cobbles and began to bleed. The man didn't notice. I had no idea where they might be headed, but if it wasn't somewhere very near, little of this animal would have been left when they got there.

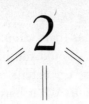

2

By NINE the next evening, La Paz was ablaze. A pall of smoke veiled the city. The air reeked of sulfur. Fires burned on every block, and explosions rocked the streets. This was la Noche de San Juan, the longest night of the year. La Paz was *en fête*.

Carmen, on furlough from Héctor till morning, had agreed to be my Ariadne. She took me into the Indian quarter, where people were packed like bees on honeycombs. The pavements, no wider than window ledges, teemed. Yet the Indian excels at accommodation, and rarely was anyone forced into the street. That was all to the good since drivers here are jealous of their turf and interlopers get short shrift.

What disruption there was, was of my making. By giving the wall when I should have taken it, and taking it when it should properly have been given, I made a shambles of their rules of precedence. I was someone with two left feet attempting a dance that would ever be beyond him.

"Look," said Carmen, pointing to a row of crones stooped over steaming caldrons. "The market women are making a cocktail. I've forgotten what it's called."

"Perhaps it's *ayahuasca*," I said.

"I've never heard of it."

"It was something the Incas drank. They said it helped them divine the future. Would you like some?"

"I don't think so. It's very potent."

"You're being a puritan. What harm can it do you?"

Carmen looked again at the row of pots. "I'd rather not," she said.

In one of the caldrons, the owner had placed a stick, which she twirled back and forth between her palms like someone making fire. The concoction in her pot began to froth. Was it my imagination, or did she cackle? *I'll get you, my pretty. And your little dog too.*

To be frank, market women unnerved me. Just that afternoon I had raised the ire of one by knocking over her pail of *refresco*, flavored water that is supposed to quench the thirst. The woman glared with such ferocity that, before I quite knew what I was doing, I had pressed all my money on her and fled!

Bolivia's merchant class, these Indian women are responsible for most of the country's trade. Yet it is not their business acumen, considerable though it is, as much as their mien that makes one quail. They view the world with a detachment approaching insensibility and seem not so much indifferent to one's presence as oblivious to it. Quite the hardest part of engaging them in commerce is gaining their attention. The annals of trade provide few examples of such insouciance.

Even their dress conspires to make them awesome. They wear—all at once—several colored skirts, a blouse, a quantity of cardigans, a pinafore, and a shawl. Silver earrings, and a derby set raffishly on the side of the head, complete the effect. It must take them an age to dress.

The shawl doubles as kit bag and papoose. It is unusual to see an Indian woman unencumbered. These bundles might be natural appendages, encumbered and encumbrance a single organism. Perhaps they provide balance. I shouldn't wonder if the experience of always carrying something on one's back wouldn't have the effect, in time, of shifting one's center of gravity.

I tried to imagine Carmen in a derby—and found I couldn't. In addition to the ill-fitting stockings billowing sadly over the sides of her shoes, she was wearing this evening a dress that flared dramatically at the knees. It gave her, I regret to say, the appearance of a cowcatcher. Her makeup was equally outlandish, her face so lavishly powdered that she might have been the victim of a flour bomb.

She boasted of having made the dress herself. "I saw it in a magazine," she said. "It's the latest fashion."

I must have looked dubious.

"It is, isn't it?" she went on.

"Quite possibly. I'm not a good person to ask about these things."

It had been arranged that we make a *fogata*, a bonfire, at the home of Carmen's Aunt Flora. A massive woman—she was more arboreal than floral—Flora met us at the door with a raised broom.

"Oh, it's you," she said crossly. "I thought you were the dog. I've just chased it out. Come in."

Flora, whom I was meeting for the first time, refused me any acknowledgment. Instead, aunt and niece chatted in Aymara, Carmen apparently explaining how she'd made her dress billow. And then the dog nosed around the door. Flora swelled with rage. "I'll wring your neck," she bellowed, charging into the courtyard. "If I get my hands on you, I'll skin you alive."

"Do you think it was wise to bring me here?" I asked Carmen, taking advantage of Flora's absence. "Your aunt seems not very glad to see me."

"Of course she is. She likes you."

"She does?"

"Yes. She said you gave her ten dollars this morning."

"Not me. She must be mistaken."

"Yes, you. You kicked over her *refresco*."

Perhaps Flora did like me, because later, during another attempt on the life of the egregious dog, her hat fell off and I managed to snatch it away before the animal could harm it. Returning it to her, I elicited my first response of the evening: a grunt. I felt enormously heartened.

Flora proved herself a good sort. For the rest of the evening, she plied me with drink.

"Do you like Carmen?" she asked at one point. She and I had just lighted a bonfire in her courtyard. Carmen had been sent to buy more liquor.

"I like her very much," I said.

"Are you going to marry her?"

"Oh, I hardly think so. Why?"

"She wants to marry a European. She's even talked of marrying an American."

"Is that why she wears those stockings?"

"She says she has no choice."

"And does she?"

Flora shrugged. "There is a lot of prejudice in this country. Indians are considered stupid and cruel and devious. That's what the whites believe, and many Indians believe it too. Sometimes, I believe it myself. If enough people think badly of you, you begin to think they must be right."

"And Carmen?"

Flora looked at the sky. The moon, full a night ago, glowed a reddish orange. "She wants a better life. She can only have it if she stops being an Indian."

She tossed a sheaf of banana leaves onto the fire. It had grown sullen. So rarefied is the air here that fire has trouble finding nourishment. La Paz makes slim pickings for the arsonist. Even so, it has its fire department. I once saw one of its trucks casually make its way to an emergency somewhere. The crew wore blue overalls and red, tin helmets. They had the air of people with time to burn.

The next time the *fogata* burned low, Flora fed it a straw mattress. Her neighbors contributed an elderly table and chair. Then a primitive gramophone was consigned to the flames. Bonfires perform some of the same functions as garage sales.

In the street children exploded cherry bombs and bottle rockets. Occasionally one would toss a firecracker at a hapless passerby. But mostly they were content to terrify one another. Later the older ones mounted bicycles and whipped around the fires with all the panache of expert skiers.

Their parents, less demonstrative, watched the flames in silence. Perhaps they were remembering the Incas, who would kindle fire in the morning to make the sun appear. Throwing maize on the hot coals, the priests would call, "Eat this, Lord Sun, and know that we are your children."

But maybe not. Religious feeling seemed absent. This was a Spanish event, after all, not an Indian one. The *fogatas* had their origin in the European fire festivals staged to mark the summer solstice. For the Bolivian Indian, the size of Europe's harvests was not of great concern.

They might, of course, have adapted the occasion, given it resonance. Surviving conditions as harsh as theirs was no mean achievement, and fire had made it possible. But Prometheus is a hero to conquerors, not to the conquered. Fire produced the tools with which the Indians subdued their environment, but it also produced the weapons with which others—the Incas, the Spanish, Bolivia's current rulers—subdued the Indians. They had little reason to esteem tech-

nology. To them, a people convinced that rebellion against
mortal fate is futile, its achievements would always be
dubious.

The *fogatas* had convinced me that I should move to the Indian
quarter. But before I did that I would have to find a hotel.
It wouldn't be easy. Accommodation in La Paz reminds one
of the two diners discussing the meal they'd just eaten: "The
food was awful," said one. "Quite," said the other. "And
there wasn't nearly enough of it."

My first choice was the Italia, which, despite its noise
levels, appealed to me because Christopher Isherwood had
once stayed there. But the Italia was full. So were the Rosario,
the Tumusla, and the Los Angeles. The Illimani was full,
the España was full, and the Andes was full. The Oruro
wasn't merely full, it was, in the words of the manager, "full
to overflowing." And the Universario expected to be full "for
at least a week."

Fortunately, I had an alternative. Flora had mentioned a
boardinghouse run by a friend of hers, Pedro. "But only in
an emergency," she had said. Ordinarily this would have
given me pause. Bolivians are inured to discomfort and assume
others are too. But evening was coming on, and the temperature had begun to drop. I had no wish to spend the night
out-of-doors.

Or did I? Pedro's *residencial* made me wonder. No soft
vicissitudes of pleasure and repose here. In my room, the
window wouldn't open, the door wouldn't close, the bed
lacked blankets, there was no hot water, and a hole under
the sink was big enough to admit a badger. What was more,
my "private" bathroom was also the family bathroom. And
Pedro had sired an extensive family.

My room's only decoration was a handwritten note pinned

to the wardrobe: "Single guests may not be visited in their rooms by members of the opposite sex, persons of doubtful moral character or animals of any species. No exceptions." If that badger ever came back, I'd be in trouble.

Uncontaminated by training, Pedro was a minimalist. Used to the worst conditions himself, he didn't consider that others might attach any greater importance to comfort than he did. But in one area he was punctilious. "I will not tolerate rats," he told me. "If you see one in your room, I want to be told immediately."

It is consoling, perhaps, that hotel standards in La Paz are not a consequence of any steady deterioration. Although many hotels are admittedly wretched, it must truthfully be said that wretched they always have been. When the writer Frank Vincent visited the city in 1890, the only hotel worthy of the name was "the Grand, kept by a Frenchman." But the Grand was not to prosper. It was still "the only decent hotel" in La Paz when Paul Walle came here in 1914, but when the botanist H. H. Rusby tried to stay there nineteen years later, the Grand had become "a pile of dust." (Just as well. Rusby had stayed at the Grand on a previous visit to Bolivia and found it a place in which "life was associated with many sights and sounds calculated to make one abjure food.")

It was one of the virtues of Pedro's that it was cheap. My room cost 10 million pesos a night—about four dollars. The extraordinary exchange rate could be blamed on inflation, which in 1985 rose a startling 4,000 percent. This inflation didn't gallop; it approached the speed of light.

At the time of my visit, a telephone call cost 250,000 pesos, a newspaper 500,000. One paid a million pesos for a beer, 2 million for a sandwich, 4 million for a light lunch. Disbursing these sums, it was hard not to feel a little giddy; wealth would be the death of me.

Pedro's only other guest was Julio, a Chilean whom I met in the courtyard next morning. Crouched over a small stove, he was making porridge.

"Want some?" he asked.

"Do you have any sugar?"

"Never touch it. It's bad for you."

"Cream?"

He shook his head.

"Then I don't think I will, thank you."

"I think you should," he said. "Eat nothing they cook here. The kitchen is filthy."

Julio claimed to be an opponent of Pinochet and said he had come to Bolivia to lie low.

"I attracted the attention of the secret police. That's not the kind of attention you want. Those people are zealots. I fear zealots."

But Julio was something of a zealot himself. He fancied himself the ascetic and practiced a self-denial which, in addition to sugarless breakfasts, also extended to sex.

"I haven't had a woman in three years," he said. "Sometimes I try to remember what a woman's like. And can't. I've forgotten."

Why did he forbear?

"Sex is bad for you. Ever wonder why you feel so tired after sex? It's because you've lost all that semen. Doesn't that tell you something?"

"What?"

"Sexual emissions dissipate the whatchamacallit." He paused. "The life force. We shouldn't be squandering our semen; we should be storing it up, accumulating it. I know what I'm talking about. I study yoga. As long as you screw, you're never going to center yourself."

Julio had a morbid dread of falling ill. In his room later he showed me the medicine chest he had brought from Santiago. A massive thing, it had contents that would have equipped a small field hospital: scissors, tweezers, cotton, gauze, adhesive tape, cleansing tissues, a thermometer, a flashlight, elastic stockings (for varicose veins), aspirin, milk of magnesia, Donnagel (for diarrhea), Nembutal (to induce sleep), a cough suppressant, Alka-Seltzer, antibiotics, antihistamines, Sucrets, Dramamine, Valium, a staggering quantity of toilet paper rolls, Desenex (for athlete's foot), Nivea, suntan oil, Anusol (for hemorrhoids), Otomide (for earaches), antimalaria tablets, insect repellent, and vitamins. Dozens of vitamins.

He imagined himself waging a war on germs. Perhaps I didn't realize the extent of the problem, he said. "Germs destroy bodies; they ruin lives. They can even alter the course of human destiny." Men didn't make history, he said; germs did. Germs raised some civilizations and cast down others. Germs defeated Hitler. Those same germs had earlier defeated Alexander and Napoleon. "The world as we know it today is entirely the work of germs."

He sounded warning after warning. I was urged to avoid fleas—they transmitted plague—and roundworms, some of which were a foot long, he said. "They work their way up the esophagus and out the mouth. People have been known to choke to death on them."

He had a special dread of lice. "The terror of the trenches," he called them. "They carry typhus." Such was this fear that once a week he squirted his clothes and body with gasoline. "That keeps them away for a while."

Julio saw himself as particularly threatened in Bolivia. "The tropics are a white man's grave, you know." He washed his vegetables in detergent, shunned water that hadn't been sterilized, and never stood when he might be lying down. "I lie flat whenever I can," he said. "It doesn't matter where I am. At this altitude especially, you must let the body relax."

When he wasn't pondering his health, he was considering his mortality. The main cemetery, high in the Indian quarter, fascinated him. It was where he spent most of his afternoons.

"An extraordinary place!" he said. "You simply have to see it. But keep your shoes on. It's full of whatchamacallit."

"Whatchamacallit?"

"Shit."

I knew about the cemetery. In *The Capitals of Spanish America*, the book he wrote in 1888, William Curtis described it as "very extensive" and "one of the finest in South America." Carmen took me there the next day. It was certainly large. And busy. In just two hours we saw five funerals—one for an adult, a second for a young child, and three for infants.

Of the last group, the first was particularly sad. The parents entered the mortuary chapel carrying between them a tiny white coffin. It was no bigger than a shoe box. A child could have borne it. The coffin was placed at the foot of the altar, and a short service followed.

The obsequies completed, the parents carried the coffin to a mausoleum in the cemetery, where two workmen placed it in a small recess. The niche was then bricked over and cemented. This took some six or seven minutes, during which the parents stood clutching each other. Neither spoke. When the recess had been closed, the father wrote the dead child's name in the wet cement. One of the workmen had handed him a stick for the purpose.

A small space existed between the wall concealing the coffin and the face of the mausoleum, and it was there that the flowers were placed. The parents had brought some lilies, but they were much too long. To make them fit, one of the workmen snapped them over his knee. The action had something brutal about it. After that the parents wandered slowly away.

Walking back to the chapel, we saw a woman give a blind man several oranges and a loaf of bread. She was enlisting him to pray for her dead husband. The prayers of the blind are thought to have a special efficacy.

"This is how he makes a living," said Carmen.

"Anything else?" he asked the widow when he'd finished. She shook her head. She was wearing brown bedroom slippers.

The chief mourners at the funeral for the adult were a group of elderly women. After the service they formed a line outside the chapel and accepted condolences. The mood was solemn, yet there was no grief. Bolivians are no strangers to death. Here one in every five babies dies at birth, and the average life expectancy is less than half a century. The Bolivian has no trouble visualizing his ultimate fate. Like Seneca, he has death constantly before him.

Their circumstances have produced in these people an awareness of their mortality reminiscent of the Middle Ages. For them death is a chance event, an inscrutable part of a universe forever outside their comprehension. It is only necessary that they learn to accept it. And they have. The Renaissance conception of the world as full of joy is not one they understand. Life is something to endure, with the consequence that death inspires no dread in them. With death comes peace.

Wandering around the mausoleums, I noticed that some of the niches had been broken open.

"Those graves have been desecrated," I said to Carmen. "La Paz has grave robbers?"

"Young boys steal the skulls," she said. "We have a skull

fiesta every year. Skulls foretell the future. The market women pray to them."

"Flora, too?"

"Flora, too. Every fiesta day, she comes here to buy skulls."

"How many?"

"It depends on how much money she has. They cost fifty cents each. Maybe six, maybe seven."

"And what does she do with them?"

"She takes them into the chapel to hear mass, and then she feeds them. It's what you would call a wake. She makes a mound of the skulls and lights candles around them."

"But how are they fed?"

"First, you give coca leaves to the skulls, and then *you* take some, which you chew on the skulls' behalf. If the leaves taste sweet, it means a good year for business. If they are sour, it means a bad year."

Sometimes, Carmen explained, her aunt gave the skulls cigarettes, after which Flora, again in the role of surrogate, smoked one herself. "White ash means good news; black ash, bad news. Maybe even death."

"Does Flora believe all this?"

"Certainly. She wears a piece of skull on a string around her neck. She says it brings her luck."

Afterward the skulls are returned to the boys who disinterred them. "They are supposed to put them back. Who knows what they do with them?"

Implicitly at least the church sanctions these practices. Historically undermanned and wielding little political influence, it never quite managed to stamp out local beliefs. A powerful clergy might have succeeded in imposing Catholic orthodoxy. Instead, with little clergy at all, the church has had to watch while the Aymara adopted only those aspects of Christianity they found palatable and ignored those they didn't. What has emerged from this process is a folk Catholicism of a particular richness. While making a show of honoring the Christian pantheon, the Indians continue to worship the gods of their fathers, reserving their special reverence for Christian icons whose attributes recall a pre-Columbian counterpart.

The world, as the Aymara see it, is not a happy place. It is hostile and dangerous and cruel. Demons fill it—demons who steal children, destroy crops, kill farm animals, drive men mad. A God extending peace and love has little chance against such adversaries. Better to rely on the magic that served their ancestors.

Carmen glanced at her watch. "I must get back to work. Señor Héctor will want his dinner. What are you doing this evening?"

"I'm off to a party."

Julio and several of his yoga friends were having a get-together, and I had been invited to join them.

"It'll be fun," Julio had assured me.

"Wine, women, and song?"

"I hardly think so," he said coldly. "These people are like me—celibate."

It sounded less than promising, but I was curious: I had never seen the semen retentive at play before.

The party was being given in an office building off the Prado, and, although I got there a little early, singing already issued from the top floor. The festivities had begun. I walked upstairs, tracing the commotion to its source, and found myself in a room of thirty swaying people. They stood with arms linked and eyes closed, their faces bearing expressions of spurious joy—the look of people who imagine themselves close to God.

I had two thoughts: Either Julio was a lot more daft than he appeared or he was having fun at my expense. Then I had a third thought: I deserve this for consorting with someone like him. And a fourth: I must get out of here. But before I could make a move, the thirty swaying bodies had sufficiently recovered themselves to become aware of me.

"Jesus loves you," they said as one. I tried to retreat into the hall, but they had me surrounded. I was being hugged and kissed from all sides. A deluge of agape. They might have loved me to death had I not managed to struggle free and bolt for the stairs.

Back on the street I noticed for the first time the two name plates on the door: The Great Universal Brotherhood, the organization to which Julio belonged, and below it this: The Jimmy Swaggart Ministry.

I found Julio back at the hotel eating a pizza.

"They canceled the party," he said. "I meant to tell you, but I forgot."

He gripped his stomach.

"What's the matter?"

"Nothing. A sudden stab of pain. It's—" He stopped.

"Is everything all right?"

"I think so. I feel a bit nauseated, and my head hurts. Probably nothing very important." He was looking deathly pale.

"My mouth has just gone dry," he said.

"Maybe I should get you upstairs," I said. "You should be lying down."

By the time I got him to his room, he was having trouble breathing. And then he began to vomit.

"I shouldn't have eaten those anchovies," he wailed. "I've been poisoned."

He began fumbling for his medical dictionary but couldn't get it open.

"I can't control my hands," he said, handing me the book.

"You do it. Look under *clupeotoxic fish poisoning*. Read me what it says."

I found the entry and began to read: "The following effects are usually rapid and violent: sharp metallic taste, nausea, dry mouth, vomiting, abdominal pain, diarrhea, chills, vertigo, low blood pressure, headache, tingling and numbness, cramps, respiratory distress, convulsions . . . Oh, God."

"What's the matter?" he said, looking frightened. "Give me that." He grabbed the book. "Let's see . . . Clupeotoxic poisoning. . . . Respiratory distress, convulsions. . . . Oh, Jesus, I'm finished. It says death often occurs within fifteen minutes. Get me a doctor. Quick!"

I raced downstairs and found Pedro in the lobby.

"Julio is very ill. He needs a doctor right away."

"What's wrong with him?"

"He has food poisoning."

"Let me see him."

Pedro took one look at Julio and made his diagnosis.

"Altitude sickness," he said. "What he needs is *mate de coca*. I'll send some up."

He was right. After a cup of *mate*, Julio grudgingly admitted to feeling better.

"That man is an alarmist," Pedro said afterward. Pedro himself wasn't given to panic. He prided himself on being prudent.

"What is the one thing that Henry Ford, Nelson Rockefeller, and Simón Patiño have in common?" he wanted to know.

"Beats me. Greed?"

"Prudence," he said, tapping his forehead. "You won't succeed in business unless you're prudent."

Pedro dreamed of business success. In addition to his hotel, he owned a truck in which, every morning, he hauled vegetables from villages on the Altiplano to the markets in La Paz. And recently he had begun staging *peñas*—concerts of Bolivian folk music.

Peñas thrived in La Paz, but Pedro didn't see them doing so for very much longer. "Bolivia is obsessed with becoming modern," he said. "The young people have no interest in the old ways. Everything is electronic. Folk music will die. Very soon now, no more *peñas*." He looked glum.

"It's very sad to see a culture fail," I offered.

"Oh, that's neither here nor there," he said. "It's the business aspect that worries me. *Peñas* are a gold mine. Tourists love them."

Tourists did love *peñas*, but not the ones Pedro organized. The one I went to was a disaster. It was also sparsely attended, something Pedro sought to disguise by filling the room with members of his family. Although the musicians that particular evening lacked any discernible talent, Pedro had placed his three teenage daughters in the front row with instructions to clap and cheer at the end of each number. Constanza, the eldest of them, had even been supplied with flowers, which she was to rain on stage when, in her opinion, a performance demanded more than mere applause.

"Like the band?" Pedro asked me during the intermission.

"I'm afraid I don't."

"Awful, aren't they? Never mind. With a little luck, the tourists won't be able to tell the difference."

Whether or not they could, we were never to know. On this occasion—and indeed on several subsequent ones—tourists were conspicuously absent. The locals, though, *did* know the difference, and they were not slow to pronounce judgment.

"Give us another," Constanza called to the performers.

And a member of the audience called out, "Better yet: Give us another group."

The music went from bad to worse, and by the time the set had finished, even Constanza and her sisters had fallen sullen. The group left the stage, hovered in the wings, and then returned to the spotlight. They played three encores. To punish us for our indifference, no doubt. And all the while Pedro's extensive family moved from table to table selling ice cream, stale cake, cotton candy, and breaded pork chops.

Afterward even Pedro admitted to being discouraged. "If it weren't for the children, I'd get out of this business altogether," he said.

But this was disingenuous. The truth was that Pedro loved money, and it was his ambition to be very rich. Besides owning a hotel and a truck, he was something of a usurer. Flora was one of his clients. She and the other market women were always in need of credit. By lending them money at high rates of interest—many could get loans nowhere else—Pedro had amassed considerable capital.

He also saw himself as a power broker. The revolution of 1952 had made the Bolivian peasant a major political force, and Pedro, who had contacts in the communities surrounding the capital, was in a position to wheel and deal. His ability to deliver a few hundred votes at election time made him important to candidates needing rural support. And the candidates were not ungrateful. Pedro's nominees filled several local offices. And he was consulted when public monies were being spent.

"I'm a good person to know," he said. "I can get things done."

He exaggerated. The offices he filled were minor, and the monies were insignificant. Yet within his small sphere, he was not without influence. With everyone, that is, except Claudia, his wife. In a fit of scruples two years earlier, Claudia had announced that she was renouncing sex and, henceforth, would model herself on St. Catherine of Siena.

"Why St. Catherine?" I asked him.

"They have a lot in common. They're both mad. Do you know anything about St. Catherine? She claimed to be a stigmata, but the wounds, she said, were visible only to her. She lived on lettuce. She told people Jesus and she were lovers. She said he wanted to marry her. He was even supposed to have given her a present—his foreskin. That woman wasn't a saint; she was a lunatic. And my wife is turning out just like her. She won't sleep with me anymore. She says I smell of sin. What am I to do? I have to have sex."

"Then have an affair."

"In La Paz? You must be joking. Extramarital sex is almost unknown."

That certainly explained the prevalence of soft-core pornography. At any one time as many as half the city's cinemas are showing titles such as *24 Hours of Pleasure*, *Suzy the Nymphomaniac*, *Island of Naked Slaves*, and *Hospital Porno*. Pedro had seen *Hospital Porno*—"These nurses have all the remedies, including one you didn't know existed," said the advertising—and he wanted to see it again.

"Great stuff," he said. "Lots of tits; lots of boom-boom. Tomorrow is my *viernes de solteros*—my night out with the boys. You come with me. We'll see it together."

Buying tickets was the best part of the evening. A model of the auditorium was displayed in the box office. This model bore two thousand tiny holes—each representing a seat—and into these minute cavities, someone had had the invidious job of placing two thousand tightly rolled pink tickets. Ticket buyers consulted the model, indicated where they wanted to sit, and took their pink slips to the auditorium, where an usher waited to show them to their seats.

The system might have worked had the auditorium not been very dark. Unable to read the tickets, the usher adopted the expedient of directing everyone to the same few rows in the center stalls, with the result that it was only after much pushing and shoving that we finally managed to seat ourselves. It all took some time, and I had ample opportunity to ponder the notice above the screen. "Censorship is not a caprice," it said, "but a necessity if we are to preserve public morality."

The film was a disappointment. To quote Pedro, there were tits galore, but no boom-boom that I could see. The protagonists were a doctor who leered a lot and a nurse with a respiratory infection. The doctor must have been a good sort because, solicitous of Nurse's health, he gave her frequent chest examinations. Thorough examinations too.

Nurse, to her credit, was very brave about the whole thing. Although she was obviously very ill, she never once complained. If anyone deserved good health it was she, but I'm unable to say if she ever recovered. She was retiring her massive mammaries after one of Doctor's periodic checkups when the projector broke down. Instead of storming the box office, the audience filed quietly into the street. They looked so solemn, they might have been people leaving church.

Perhaps they went to the used-book stalls on Montes Avenue, where pornography posed as educational material: *The ABC of Sex, The Sex Atlas, The Sex Compendium, The Dictionary of Sex*. The language was scientific, the tone prurient. And the illustrations featured naked, romping children. Or maybe they perused, in a window across the street, photographs of a recent beauty pageant. The contestants—not a good-looking face among them—wore swimsuits of surprising brevity, the legs cut very high, the crotch very narrow. The effect was oddly lewd.

"This is the Spanish legacy," said Pedro, turning sadly away from these pictures. "This is what asceticism has done to us."

The struggle against concupiscence has produced in this country a horror of sexuality. Out of the dualism that pitted soul and body against each other has emerged an antipathy for sex unusual in its vigor. Pedro found himself inadequate to its austerities.

"There's no sex before marriage in Bolivia," he said. "And in my case, no sex after marriage. What is a man to do? Self-discipline is one thing, but unnecessary denial is going too far. Pleasure isn't bad, is it?"

"Not unless pain is good."

"You know that fellow Julio? He tried to tell me the other day that it's good to suffer. He says he's celibate. What man in his right mind would be celibate? He's a fruitcake!"

I had begun to think Pedro right. Julio's behavior had become increasingly erratic. Just yesterday he had stripped his room of wallpaper because, he said, fleas were breeding behind it. And getting back to the hotel after *Hospital Porno*, I found that he had taken to his bed. He had developed foot blisters.

"I may never walk again," he said.

"Oh, they can't be that serious. Isn't there something you can put on them?"

"Boric acid would help."

"Well, what's the problem?"

"I don't have any. Do you think you could get me some?"

That was relatively easy. Finding anything in the La Paz markets is facilitated by their medieval character. As in the cities of the Middle Ages, each trade has its own locale. A strict division is observed: apples on one block, oranges on another; here for potatoes, there for onions. There is a street for tomatoes, which are usually sold in conjunction with carrots, and another for coca leaves—sacks and sacks of them. Yams, corn, lettuce, beets, cabbage, beans, and peas—each in its appointed place.

Trade has a hierarchy. At the top are those women who own their own stores; at the bottom, vendors selling a single product. It is commerce at its most rudimentary: a dozen tubes of toothpaste, a small mound of tangerines, several boxes of handkerchiefs, a bundle of ballpoint pens, a few packets of Alka-Seltzer. One woman I saw had a scale on which, for a small fee, one might weigh oneself; another offered the public the use of a telephone that she kept covered with something resembling a poorly fashioned tea cozy.

It isn't just the markets here that remind one of the four-teenth century. Feudal too is the contempt for cleanliness. People eliminate in the streets at will. In some areas signs urge one not to spit, while in others the prohibition is on urinating. In others still it is defecating that is forbidden. (I saw no sign that forbade all three.) All for naught. Bolivians, exercising that love of freedom which is their special charm, spit and piss and shit as whimsy dictates.

Some days there can be as many as twenty thousand vendors in La Paz, and they sell everything from shrunken heads to dried embryos. What they don't sell—and I can say this with some authority because I scoured the city for one—is cocktail shakers. I was rather cross about it. I was planning an ex-pedition to Laja, Héctor's country seat until 1952, when his-tory brought him low. Now I would have to reconsider.

Héctor hadn't been encouraging when I'd mentioned my intentions. "*You* on the Altiplano?" he said. "You're a fool. What will you eat? Where will you sleep? You'll die of cold. It's folly. Sheer folly."

He was doubtless right. Which gave me no alternative. There could be no going back. Cocktail shaker or no, the trip would have to be prosecuted.

I spent my last day in La Paz outfitting myself. The morning went well, most of the foodstuffs I wanted—raisins, nuts, sugar, coffee, dried milk, chocolate, pasta, and packet soups—being found fairly readily in the markets. The afternoon was more difficult. I had now to locate water-sterilization tablets, and my inquiries yielded nothing. "Purify water?" said one woman. "Why would you want to do that?"

Crossing the Altiplano without a martini was feasible. Without potable water it was out of the question. That's it then, I thought. Laja will have to wait.

Not so. Walking back to Pedro's, I was overtaken by three English students, each clutching a Penguin Classic: *The Treasure of the City of Ladies* by Christine de Pisan, *The History and Topography of Ireland* by Gerald of Wales, and Justinian's *Digest of Roman Law*. Obviously exhausted, they had come off a train three hours earlier and had spent the time since looking for a hotel. They were embarrassingly grateful when I mentioned Pedro's.

"It's not listed in any of our guides," said Christine de Pisan.

"It hasn't been discovered yet," I said. "Though that could change at any moment."

"Then we'd best get down there right away," said Gerald of Wales.

"Very decent of you," said Justinian. "I wish there was something we could do for you."

"Well, there probably is," I said. "Can you spare any sterilization tablets?"

They could. Which left me with just candles to buy. Oh, and I would have to have my shoes repaired. La Paz's cobbles had pried loose the soles.

3

THE ALTIPLANO is 1,000 feet above La Paz, and Pedro and I began our climb the next morning. It was slow going. Up, up, we went, the vast tableland, it seemed, getting no closer. More than once I considered turning back. Out of the question! I couldn't let this defeat me.

We pressed on, La Paz dropping farther and farther behind us. I was sweating badly and had a choking thirst. The sun was directly overhead. This was madness. But there could be no stopping now. Let Pedro give up, I thought; I never would. I struggled on, instinct alone keeping me going. I remember little of the last 200 feet. I was no longer thinking.

"We're here," Pedro said at last. I was about to drop. We were 3 miles above sea level. Had I not been riding in his truck, I never would have made it.

"Tell me again where Laja is," I said when he dropped me off. He had vegetables to collect.

"It's northwest," he said, pointing across the treeless plain. "Over there."

There was nothing "over there" that I could see. There was nothing anywhere. Just an arid expanse of red earth, a great void, 40,000 square miles of emptiness.

"Good God," I said. "A trackless waste."

"Not entirely," said Pedro. He was not in good spirits. Last night's *peña* had drawn no audience at all. "There's the main road. You can take a bus."

"I'd rather walk. If I hurry, I can be there by nightfall."

"Then stay on this road," he said. "And don't forget, it gets very cold when the sun sets. Watch out for those frosts."

I set forth, just a little uncomfortable. It was the size of the place. It is too big. The scale is wrong. All that nullity. This barren plain and above it a sky that soars and soars. It seems limitless. I imagined it extending deep into space, leaving the world far behind, thrusting farther and farther into infinity. Not a cloud in it. Not a bird. Why on earth would people have settled here? What could have drawn them to a place that so belittles them?

There were llamas, sheep, some cows, the occasional homestead. The last were widely scattered. The poverty of the land—much of it is poisoned by borax—precludes proximity. The homes, small and often windowless, looked sullen. Each had a walled yard—a pen for livestock. This mud-brick architecture was depressingly tentative. The sun had made it friable. A precipitous action, I couldn't help thinking—a slammed door, a raised voice—and it would crumble. Dust unto dust.

Most of the homes seemed deserted. I saw just three people all morning. Women, they scuttled out-of-doors for a moment, glanced around, and scuttled back in again. There was just a hint of panic about them. Perhaps they felt safer inside.

I trudged on, the baked earth rising in clouds around me. The road wove across the plateau in wide loops. And then it did something I hadn't anticipated. It divided. Not a great divide, by any means, but a divide nonetheless. Where one had been, now there were two. And both seemed to head northwest. To one extent or another. But then I really didn't

know where northwest was. I had a general idea. If I wasn't
to lose myself, that was hardly enough.

I felt suddenly reckless. What did it matter which road I
took? In a place as vast and bleak as this, decisions were of
no account. Right or left, ultimately it was of no consequence.
Here all one could do was trust to fate.

My indifference startled me. This was no small matter,
after all. Take a wrong turn and I might die of exposure. But
beyond admitting this to myself, I couldn't be terribly interested. I felt curiously helpless. This windswept tundra defied
one's best efforts. It would not be controlled. I felt dwarfed,
robbed of significance. Robbed of significance and freed of
responsibility. I didn't matter, nor did anything I might do.

I changed my tune when the sun set. It happened before
I knew it. One minute the sun was there; the next, the
shadow of the mountains fell across me, and it had gone.
Almost immediately the wind picked up. A chill ran through
me. In fifteen minutes it would be dark. I had a quarter of
an hour to find shelter if I wasn't to die of cold.

I checked my pockets. Yes, I had my passport. At least my
relatives would be told of my demise. How angry I'd make
them; dying miles from anywhere was hardly considerate.
There would be the cost of shipping my body home. And
there would be customs inspections and papers to complete.
There might even be duties to pay. What a lot of bother!

But I was to be spared. At least for the time being. There,
ahead of me, was an abandoned hut. It lacked a door, and
part of the roof had fallen in, but it would do. Thank goodness
I'd brought a sleeping bag. The night would be long, but I
would no doubt survive it.

The sky began to fill with stars. Wonderful things, they
burned so fiercely I could almost hear them crackle. Doughty
loved the stars, loved to lie awake and watch them as I was
doing now. Under the stars, he said, he found "more refresh-

ment than upon beds and pillows in our close chambers." My
back began to ache. What I would have given just then for
a chamber, however close. What I would have given for one
of Pedro's flea pits.

I woke as the sun came up. Something wet had brushed
across my face. A pig was standing over me. It nudged me
again. And then it fled, squealing in terror. I don't look my
best in the morning.

A man looked around the door. "Did you hit it?" he asked.

"I didn't lay a hand on it."

"Well, you should have," he said. "That animal is a thorn
in my side." He stepped into the hut. "My name is Marco.
Are you a Mormon?"

He looked disappointed when I shook my head.

"I met a Mormon last year," he said. "He gave me a radio."
He grinned. "You should have seen the look on that pig's
face."

The grin surprised me. Indians, I had been told by Héctor,
rarely smiled. "In all the years I've known them," Héctor
said, "I've seen them laugh maybe half a dozen times."

Marco sat down slowly. A small man, he was wearing
trousers, a white shirt, and a knitted woolen cap. The cap
had flaps, which had been pulled up to project alarmingly
from behind his ears.

"I'm drunk," he said. "Do you mind?"

"Not at all."

"Today, my brother is getting married. I've been celebrat-
ing for a week. You want to eat?"

"A cup of coffee would be nice."

"My wife will make you breakfast."

Their home consisted of a single room, the only furniture
a table, several chairs, and a bed, which Marco shared with
his wife and two children. Decoration was absent. There

were no pictures on the walls, no cloth on the table, no cushions on the chairs. On the floor, no covering of any sort. The newspaper pinned above the bed was there not to provide embellishment but to exclude the cold.

The place was unkempt and poverty alone didn't explain it. Refinement is within the means of people even as poor as these. Yet nothing here had been enhanced. Their home provided them with little more than basic shelter. That was all they asked of it.

Marco's wife was cooking at a spirit stove. A massive woman, she dwarfed him. Beside her, he looked like a tiny tug fussing around the bow of the *Normandie*. She paid me no heed, and her husband neither introduced me nor made any effort to explain my presence. For all she knew, I might have materialized from one of the many beer bottles strewn around their yard.

We had potatoes for breakfast. The Altiplano Indians domesticated the potato four thousand years ago. They were the first agriculturalists in the world to do so. If they hadn't, the history of this area would certainly have been different. Because maize doesn't grow at this altitude, the early settlers, without the potato to sustain them, could never have survived. The Altiplano would have been abandoned, and the great civilization of Tiahuanaco would never have existed.

"Do you have potatoes in England?" Marco asked.

"Rather a lot," I said.

Marco's children joined us at the table. His eight-year-old daughter dispatched a fried egg and then began to read aloud from a schoolbook. Her mother, herself illiterate, listened in astonishment. Breakfast for the second child—Luis, a boy of two—consisted of mother's milk. Children on the Altiplano are suckled until they are three or four, making especially strong the bond between mother and child.

Marco referred to the boy as "my little man."

"He had his first haircut yesterday," he said. "He's no longer a baby."

Luis had been coughing since I arrived. He seemed very ill. His mother handed him an orange she had peeled. He grasped it tightly for a moment, and then his grip slackened and it fell to the floor. More coughing. I feared for him. Perhaps he had bronchitis.

"Has he seen a doctor?" I asked Marco.

"He's all right," he said.

"He seems very sick."

"He'll be fine. Come. Help me feed the pigs."

Besides his pigs, Marco kept a flock of llamas.

"Don't go near him," he said when I tried to stroke one of them. "He'll spit."

"How big is your farm?" I asked.

"Ten hectares. I grow enough to feed the family. Sometimes, there's a little left to sell."

But on a holding this size he might produce a considerable surplus, I suggested.

"Why bother?" he wanted to know.

"Well, you might want to buy a tractor. Or build a larger house. Or make the one you have more comfortable."

He shook his head. "We have everything we need," he said.

Possessions didn't interest Marco. He had made a virtue of renunciation. He had had to, he said. His survival depended on it.

"You think my home is poor, don't you?"

"No. Well . . ."

"Of course you do. So did the Mormon. But it is poor for a reason. Look around you. See how thin my pigs are? This is a poor place. The soil is poor, the grass is poor. Here, if everyone is to have something, no one can have very much.

A little is enough for us. If it weren't, we would perish."

Material possessions were not the only prosperity, he said. "I have my family and my friends. What more could anyone want?"

When we went indoors, a kettle was steaming on the stove. Water at this altitude boils at 189 degrees. Taking care to ensure that his wife didn't see him, Marco poured himself a glass of Singani. He winked elaborately and poured a glass for me. He raised a finger to his lips. He seemed a little afraid of her. Perhaps she beat him. Héctor had said it was not uncommon. Aymara wives often beat their men, he said, but rarely will a man return the violence. I could see why. Raise a hand to one of these weaker vessels, and she's likely to break your arm.

Marco's wife put a cup on the table.

"Does he want coffee?" she asked him.

"Do you want coffee?" he said, turning to me.

"Yes, please."

"Yes, he does," he told her.

Their kindness surprised me. Based on what I'd read of him, I had expected the Indian to be a nasty specimen. Redcliffe Salaman, whose history of the potato is still a classic, found him dour, cruel, and suspicious. He was more than dour, said the normally reliable Harold Osborne; he was, as well, resentful and taciturn.

A. F. Tschiffely complained that the Indian was "sulky and sullen." (Tschiffely can't have liked people very much. His book *Southern Cross to Pole Star* is dedicated to a horse.) Harry Franck accused the Indian of lacking affection, which it might have been possible to overlook if he weren't also "all too capable of bestial lust." Besides being vindictive, Paul Walle's Indian drank to excess. But then, Walle sighed, "it is characteristic of brown and black people that they do not know when to stop." Hiram Bingham, who had still to discover Machu Picchu, made a more serious charge. The Aymara, he said, were deficient, not only morally but mentally too.

And what of Bolivians themselves? How have they presented the Indian? Manuel Paredes deemed him suspicious and pessimistic, while Alcides Arguedas found him spiteful, hypocritical, cheerless, and not terribly bright. Arguedas has often been accused of racism. The 1937 edition of his *Pueblo Enfermo* (A Sick People) frequently cites *Mein Kampf*.

Many of these impressions were based not on personal experience but on accounts of the Indian provided by *patrones* and *hacendados*. Their inaccuracy then is no surprise. What *does* startle is that the Indian *wouldn't* be the ruffian described by his detractors.

An environment as grudging as the Altiplano might be expected to make its inhabitants equally grudging. And then there is the Indians' less than happy history. The regimes that flourished in this part of South America depended on a docile peasantry. When pliancy was not forthcoming, it was exacted—often very brutally.

Luis began to cough again, this time bringing up a quantity of mucus. His mother collected the phlegm in a handkerchief, which she folded and handed to Marco without looking at him.

Marco stood up. "It's time we got going," he said.

"Is your wife coming?" I asked.

"No. She has *chuño* to make."

Making *chuño*, freeze-dried potatoes, is a long process. First, the potatoes must be immersed in water for several days, after which they are exposed to the elements. To extract what water remains, the potatoes are then trod underfoot—an action reminiscent of the French peasant stomping his grapes. The *chuño* have now been dehydrated and may be stored indefinitely.

Marco's brother lived in a small town five miles away, and it was there the wedding would occur. We set out on foot.

"Do you like weddings?" asked Marco.

"Other people's," I said.

"This will be a good one. Not the kind of wedding you see in La Paz. This will be an *Indian* wedding. I'm glad you're coming. I want you to see the Aymara enjoy themselves."

We had been walking over an hour when he took a handkerchief from his pocket. It was the one his wife had given him. Then, stooping, he hid it behind a rock.

"My wife is superstitious," he said, looking embarrassed. "This is how she hopes to make Luis better."

"How?"

"Whatever is making him sick is in the handkerchief. The next person to pass here will take the sickness with him."

"Is that kind?"

"It doesn't matter. If he wishes, he can pass the sickness along to someone else. Just as I did."

"And suppose it doesn't work? Suppose Luis doesn't get better?"

"You mean if he dies? If he dies, he dies." He pointed. "You see that town? That's Pucarani. That's where we're going."

Pucarani flanks a low hill and boasts a clinic, a school, and a church. The church was full when we arrived, the pews decorated with white crepe paper, Easter lilies, and lighted candles.

The mass had advanced as far as the Sanctus when the bridal pair made their entrance. The groom walked up the aisle first, accompanied by his wedding godmother. Close behind was the bride, escorted by her wedding godfather and two little girls carrying baskets of petals.

The godparents combined the roles of guardian and watchdog. Should the young couple ever need help, the godparents had a duty to provide it. And should bride and groom ever shirk their new responsibilities, it was their godparents who would demand a reckoning.

The bride and groom looked petrified, the bride staring ahead of her even when her husband placed the ring on her finger. It must have been a little small; he had to push to get it past the knuckle. The ceremony finished with the priest taking a scapular from the neck of the bride and placing it around the neck of the groom. They were now bound together for life. There was no music and no ritual kiss.

Outside the church the party assembled in the usual configurations for photographs. Well-wishers didn't throw confetti; they placed it in handfuls on the heads of the newlyweds. The bride was now sufficiently relaxed to smile at her two tiny flower girls, their baskets still full. Neither had remembered to strew the petals.

The groom being delayed for a moment, the bride took her place in the taxi that would transport her and her husband to the wedding reception. While she waited a street peddler tried to sell her chewing gum.

"That's the formalities over," said Marco. "Now we can get down to business." By "business," I was to gather, he meant the Indian aspects of this ceremony.

The reception was being held at the home of the bride's parents. We were played into the yard by a band notable for its lack of skill. The newlyweds sat beneath a wedding bower in front of the house. With them were their godparents. The bower was draped in white. "White represents happiness," said Marco.

Almost immediately we were served a lunch of roast guinea pig. And immediately after that the bride's father approached the bower and with great ceremony presented the newlyweds with a *wayq'a*, a basket of bread and fruit. This represented his endorsement of the match, and custom demanded that bride and groom eat it then and there. Afterward the groom was seen to loosen his belt. The bride, who had no such recourse, looked, I thought, a little pale.

Drink was now pressed on everyone—Singani or *chicha*, the latter made from maize and tasting like an especially sour yogurt. "Do you know what heaven is?" asked Marco. "It's a place where you can drink *chicha* day in, day out, and never get drunk."

Then, each in turn, the guests presented their gifts—more *wayq'a* for the most part. But there were, too, numerous pails of colored plastic and a startling quantity of water tumblers. Marco had brought along some money, which he offered in an envelope bearing his name.

As each gift was accepted, it was recorded by the bride's brother in a large copybook. That done, the guest was formally thanked. First he was given a drink by the father of the bride, followed by one from the bride's mother. Then each of the groom's parents gave him a drink, after which it was the turn of the godparents.

Despite making a great effort to remain upright, the guest was now swaying dangerously. But they hadn't done with him yet. The newlyweds hadn't shown their appreciation. More drink was pressed on him—though *pressed* isn't quite right; he was now so compliant he'd have let you pull every tooth in his head.

It seemed an immoderate response to the receipt of six water glasses, and I was glad I hadn't brought anything. There's such a thing as too much gratitude. Yet declining any of these drinks would have been unthinkable. The offer of a drink is an expression of regard, and refusal is tantamount to insult. An exception is made only in the case of the bride's mother, who may pour what she's given into a flask concealed in her shawl.

Why this would be so, no one really knew. One woman

suggested that since the bride's mother was the hostess, getting drunk would be an abdication of responsibility. Another said *someone* had to keep her wits about her. In case an emergency presented itself. Marco took a more sinister view. If she didn't stay sober, he said, her guests would steal everything in sight.

More guinea pig was passed around.

"This must be costing a fortune," I remarked. "Are Indian weddings always so elaborate?"

"This is one of the better ones," said Marco. "The bride's father owns eighty or ninety llamas. He's rich."

People were losing their reserve, talking volubly, scampering around the yard, embracing one another, roaring with laughter. A couple began to dance. An ungainly shuffle. Humanity disporting itself is rarely pretty. A bottle shattered. A baby wailed. And all the while the band kept up its infernal racket. An astonishing din, which stopped suddenly when the bride screamed.

One of the guests—the groom's former girlfriend—had just produced a ring he'd given her some years earlier. As Marco explained it, this boded ill for the marriage, because the former lover could now secure the groom's demise any time she pleased. By destroying the ring, she could destroy him too. This cast a pall on the proceedings. Although the old girlfriend assured everyone that she meant the newlyweds no harm and kept the ring only out of sentiment, an element of uncertainty had been introduced.

Marco blamed the groom, saying he had been dangerously indiscreet. Not only should he have remembered giving the ring but also he should have remembered to demand it back. But most of the others faulted the former lover, describing her as jealous and spiteful. "She never forgave him for jilting her," said one man. "She's been planning this for months."

The animosity she stirred may have surprised her. At any

rate, she relented suddenly, and the ring was returned. The party revived immediately. The day had been saved.

It was time to eat again. More guinea pig, although we hardly did it justice. For most of us the simple action of raising a fork was beyond our abilities. Marco, sunk in a stupor, stared at his plate as if trying to recall when he'd last seen anything remotely like it. (The next morning he remembered nothing of the meal. It was very bad form, he complained, that our hosts hadn't provided supper.)

After dinner the party in the bower got to its feet. We raised our glasses in a toast, and the newlyweds withdrew. Marco passed around quids of coca, and shortly afterward peace descended.

Early the next morning the newlyweds again took up their position in the bower, and the festivities resumed. With their wedding night behind them, I would have expected some sign of intimacy. Instead, staring straight ahead of them, they took no more notice of each other than they had twenty-four hours earlier.

It was a day of few surprises. We sang and drank, and talked and drank, and danced and drank, and ate and drank. Drinking even punctuated drinking, people intruding on toasts to propose toasts of their own and themselves being intruded on by others with *their* toasts until finally no one really knew to whom or what he was drinking and, I would safely guess, didn't care one way or the other.

For the first time since the celebrations began, the newlyweds were now drinking too. The groom began to unbend. Toasting his guests, he said he couldn't remember when he had last enjoyed himself so much, and he hoped that all of us would come to his next wedding, which, he assured us, would be sometime very soon.

Later, begging our permission, he said he had to leave. He was halfway across the yard when he stopped short. Then, glancing back at his astonished wife, he sighed deeply and fell flat on his face. The man was soused.

The band played on. It played more loudly than I could ever have imagined. All four players were completely without talent, yet I made the mistake of exciting their expectations. I had mentioned Pedro's *peñas*, meaning only that I would put in a word for them. They took this to mean that I had now taken it on myself to guide their careers. "We'll practice," one of them assured me. "We'll practice day and night, if we have to. We won't let you down."

I woke the following morning with a splitting headache. I wouldn't survive a third day of revelry; I had to leave. Marco was in a deep sleep, and I couldn't rouse him to say goodbye. I'll take a short walk, I thought. He'll be awake when I get back.

I had been walking twenty minutes when a truck drew up beside me. "*Las ruinas?*" said the driver. "The ruins?"

I had no idea what he was talking about, but I was suddenly very tired. Instead of reviving me, the walk had exhausted the little strength I had left. I wanted very badly to sit down and never move again. The cab looked irresistible.

"*Las ruinas,*" I said, climbing in.

But if I'd hoped to sleep, I was disappointed. The ride was excruciating. Little of the road was paved, and we were shaken around horribly. One jolt would throw the head back and force the mouth open; then, seconds later, another jolt would slam the mouth shut.

The drive was uphill much of the way. Too uphill, I thought, for our aging truck. The driver seemed to share my apprehension. He blessed himself a lot and frequently referred to an instruction manual. We forded a river. Then, mercifully, I fell asleep.

Sometime later the driver shook me awake. "The ruins," he said.

"Excellent," I answered and prepared to go back to sleep.

"The ruins," he repeated. "We are here."

"Where?"

"At Tiahuanaco."

So little remains of Tiahuanaco that today it is easy to miss. Yet a thousand years ago there was centered here one of the most advanced Indian civilizations ever to exist in South America. Ruled by priests, this theocratic state extended its influence throughout the Andes and extracted tribute from less powerful cultures in many parts of the continent. Yet for all its achievement it is something of a mystery. Tiahuanaco, it is thought, came to maturity about A.D. 600, flourished for five centuries, and then disappeared. Just why has still to be determined. The state lacked a written tradition, and the archaeological record is incomplete. Nor do the Incas tell us much.

Tiahuanaco lay in ruins when the Incas discovered it in the 1400s. But the local Indians would have known about it. They had their oral histories. Is it possible that they kept this knowledge to themselves? That somehow the Incas' assiduous historians failed to uncover it? It seems unlikely. Why then does Tiahuanaco figure little in Inca legend?

True, the Incas, still consolidating their rule, saw little gain in extolling Tiahuanaco's accomplishments. But politics only partly explains the reticence. Inca control of the Altiplano, after all, was never seriously threatened. No, something larger, more concerted may have been involved: an attempt, for reasons still unclear, to wipe Tiahuanaco from the record.

The site didn't much interest the Spanish. They smashed many of its monoliths, hoping to find gold in them. They didn't, and Tiahuanaco was forgotten. In time it became an Indian cemetery. A traveler who visited the site in 1877 saw a pack of wild dogs gorging on the body of a dead child. Told of this, the local cleric shrugged. "What does it matter?" he said. "All Indians are brutes at best."

Until recently, much fantasy surrounded this place. H. S. Bellamy said Tiahuanaco proves that a satellite larger than our present moon once encircled the earth, a discovery he generously described as perhaps "the greatest achievement of modern times." Others have called Tiahuanaco the oldest civilization in the world. Bruno Oetteking, an American, said human life originated here. Tiahuanaco, he claimed, was "the enchanted spot where Indian legend, as well as archaeological proof, place the primacy of human settlement and culture, not only of the western hemisphere, but of our planet."

Oetteking had a kindred spirit in Arthur Posnansky, who rejected the "legend" of immigration across the Bering Strait. Tiahuanaco did not derive from outside the Western Hemisphere, he said, it was indigenous to it. Posnansky convinced himself that in Tiahuanaco he had found America's Garden of Eden.

Today part of Tiahuanaco has been restored: a rectangular platform walled by sandstone blocks, a subterranean temple, and the Gate of the Sun, elaborately carved in low relief and weighing many tons. Together they suggest what H. G. Wells would have called a community of obedience, a society that demanded of its members total conformity.

Those who lived here were not what is normally considered free. But they may have enjoyed what D. H. Lawrence called the greater freedom of belonging to a living, believing community—a community "active in fulfilling some unfulfilled, perhaps unrealized, purpose." Would Lawrence have liked it here? I expect so. This is a holy place. One feels it immediately. Silence grips the site, a deep silence. Everything is so quiet, the globe might suddenly have ceased to rotate, stopped in its tracks, brought up short. Listening. Completely absorbed as it strains to hear something. Intent, caring about nothing else. Just this massive concentration of effort as it listens. The world all ears. A satellite dish. Waiting for a murmur of affirmation.

The sun watching. The sun which, in Tiahuanaco legend, was borne across the sky every day by a giant condor. The sun Lawrence worshiped as the great living source of life.

The sun drew Lawrence to Taos as it had drawn him to Italy and Australia and Mexico. He craved the sun—and not merely because his health demanded it. Man's supreme moment, he said, occurs when he "looks up and is with the sun . . . as a woman is with a child." He spent his life escaping the sunless North, where myth had yielded to science and God had died of boredom. By making the world a machine, the North had killed the "inward sun of life." It had imperiled its own soul.

Not so the Indian. The Indian might yet save us. Save America at least. "Americans," said Lawrence, "must take up life where the red Indian, the Aztec, the Maya, the Inca left it off." The Indian respects nature and is sensitive to its mysteries. He is an animist. For him everything lives. When an Aymara sees the Andes, I had heard it said, he removes his hat. On the Altiplano, man and earth are one.

Yet I doubt that Lawrence would have admired the Aymara. Not for long anyway. Their inertia would have shocked him. As he had done of peasants elsewhere, he would have denounced their "utterly blank minds, crying their speech as crows cry, and living their lives as lizards among the rocks."

To attain to anything requires an ability to act, and in that the Altiplano Indians are completely lacking. They are reconciled to misery. They have become apathetic to the extent, in Marco's case, of letting his son die, if this was what fate decided.

These Indians, descended from the founders of Tiahuanaco, have degenerated. While Marco might claim to make a virtue of necessity, more telling was his lack of imagination. Anything beyond his immediate vicinity was of no interest to him. The Aymara have distanced themselves from the world, and their culture has atrophied.

The 1952 revolution might have been expected to change this, but it hadn't. The Indian today is as marginal a figure as he ever was. Marco had never been to La Paz—30 miles away. And he farmed as his ancestors had—his plow was the sort in use along the Nile before the pyramids were built.

The revolution ended the Indian's exploitation, but it did little to change his ways. He might now own land, but in the absence of credit and technical assistance, his farming methods remained pre-modern. Lacking money, the government may have hoped that the Indians themselves would modernize the nation's agriculture. But it proved a task for which they lacked the temperament. By giving them the land they had so long craved, the revolution merely reinforced the Indians' isolationism. Once again, they had something to lose, and it gave them more reason than ever to keep the world at bay.

4

N ECESSITY brought me to Oruro. From there buses go
to Siglo Veinte. But as it happened I was glad I came. Oruro
is completely lacking in what are called attractions. And I
was grateful. With nothing to see, I was freed from a con-
straint that too often makes travel merely onerous: the obli-
gation to pursue the curious, to seek out the unique.

Uniqueness is overrated—is the world's largest potato all
that compelling?—and curiosity has its dangers. Who could
forget Leonardo waiting impatiently for a dying man to expire
that he might extract his arteries? Or the ailing Dürer setting
out for Zeeland to see a beached whale, which, by the time
he got there, had decomposed? Dürer was soon to decompose
himself. The trip proved the death of him.

In Oruro there are no homes of obscure patriots to visit,
no sites on which dubious proclamations had been made.
There are no colonial paintings which, had they any merit,
would have been spirited to Spain, and no museums filled
with poor likenesses of Bolívar and dueling pistols once the
property of former heads of state.

Oruro disdains such fripperies, which meant that I was
free to wander as I would, compelled for form's sake to curse

the absence of amenities but actually feeling better than I had in weeks. Under the circumstances, the tourist booth near the main square seemed frivolous, although happily it was rarely open. But visit it anyway, because across the street is a monument to the founder of Bolivia's railway system. It is not something for which many would want to be remembered. Bolivian trains are old, erratic, and prey to every ill to which technology is heir. Rather than being commemorated in bronze, their founder should be burned in effigy.

"People come here for Carnival every year, and that's it," said Edmundo, the bank official who changed my traveler's check. "Oruro just doesn't have that many attractions. Or, I should say, it has attractions, but they're not here, if you know what I mean."

"I'm afraid I don't."

"They're somewhere else."

"You're being elliptical. Give me an example."

"Well, Huanuni is interesting, but it's thirty miles away. And Lake Poopó is worth seeing, but that's even further."

He also recommended the mineral baths at Pazña, although reaching them would entail a three-hour car journey. Or, should I be staying any length of time, I should see—indeed I should not miss—Chipaya, an Indian settlement. Journey time: eight hours. He neglected to mention that the Indians don't much like tourists and had constructed a roadblock to keep them out.

"They're all a little far," I said. "There's nothing in Oruro itself?"

"Well, there's the zoo. But I don't recommend it. It's pretty dismal. You might try the Casa de Cultura. It belonged to Simón Patiño, the tin baron, until the state took it over. But be warned: It's almost always shut."

That may be for safety reasons. The *casa* was in need of repair. When Bolivia inherited it, it can't have realized that, in addition to owning it, it would be responsible for the building's upkeep. Many blamed Patiño for the structure's decay. It was, they seemed to think, further evidence of his perfidy.

In modern Bolivia few men are more reviled. In the popular imagination Patiño is a scoundrel who stole from starving Indians, an illiterate *cholo* who bribed public officials and sabotaged the efforts of his rivals, a criminal who valued money more than he did the lives of those who worked for him.

Actually Patiño was a man of keen intelligence whose success was the result of acumen as well as fraud. In 1894 he bought his first mine with money provided by his wife. It would prove to be immensely rich, largely because of his progressiveness. One of the first to embrace mechanization, he made his mine the most modern in the country and emerged, ten years later, as Bolivia's preeminent tin miner.

Now forty-four, Patiño sought a larger theater for his efforts. He moved to Europe, where his acumen proved no less formidable. By the time he died in 1947, he dominated the tin industry on five continents.

Patiño's formula was a simple one: cut costs and increase production. What made him different was the ferocity with which the formula was applied. The wages he paid were low even by Bolivian standards; his miners worked in appalling conditions for eighty-five cents a day. Their wives and children—employed in a variety of tasks aboveground—received even less.

Strikes were frequent and were put down ruthlessly, often with the help of the national army. In one such action, the event known as the Catavi Massacre, hundreds of people lost their lives. Many were women and children.

It is not Patiño's role in that massacre that Bolivians resent so much. Or his rapacity. Or even his lack of scruples. What they cannot forgive is his decision in 1920 to leave Bolivia and live overseas. And although he would serve as his country's ambassador to France until his death, he never once returned. To a country with a deep sense of its own inferiority, this was unpardonable. Bolivia felt betrayed.

It felt betrayed again in 1952, when the mines were nationalized. By then Patiño's Bolivian interests were of small account, but his heirs demanded compensation anyway. With Washington's assistance, they pressed their case, forcing the new government to pay them $8 million—far more than the mines were worth. This offended the nationalism even of those who opposed the revolution, and when a son of Patiño visited Bolivia in 1968, angry students doused him in pig's blood.

"You should have come to Oruro when it was a major mining center," said Edmundo when I next changed a check.

"When was that?"

"Two centuries ago. It was quite a place. The most violent city in Bolivia." His eyes shone. "Completely lawless. Men were killed in broad daylight. Gangs battled in the streets. Life was cheap. Just like Tombstone. How wonderful it must have been!"

A picture of President Víctor Paz Estenssoro smiled from the wall behind him. An odd smile. Only the lower teeth were visible. This is the face one makes when the dentist asks to see one's overbite. Paz Estenssoro looked curiously apprehensive, gripping his chair as if he expected it to pitch him onto the floor.

"I get off in ten minutes," Edmundo said. "I'll take you to see the flamingos."

"What flamingos?"

"On Lake Uru Uru. There are hundreds and hundreds of them. They're famous."

Edmundo's car had a coffin strapped to the roof. He made

no mention of it, and I didn't either. I could only hope there was no one in it.

"I wonder where they can be?" he said when we came in sight of the lake. The flamingos were nowhere to be seen. "Maybe they're on the other side."

It took us an hour to find them. And not the promised hundreds either. At most, there were a dozen. But how beautiful they were. They picked around in the shallow water, sometimes rising into the air for a moment before settling back again, drawing up their legs beneath them as they did so, and folding their wings with a care that was exquisite. Several had bursts of scarlet on their chests.

The water was a royal blue, and growing through it was a grass the color of August wheat. A cow waded into the lake and began to drink. A vulture settled on its back and gazed at the line of crumpled, pink hills far in the distance.

Edmundo was getting restless. "Let's eat something," he said.

The restaurant to which he took me was ill prepared for us. After we placed our order, the kitchen staff was dispatched on a variety of errands, one to buy meat, a second for potatoes, a third for bread. They had still to return when the waiter erased the menu prices—written in chalk on a large blackboard—and replaced them with others considerably higher. Obviously it would be necessary to eat as quickly as possible.

At the cash desk a woman picked sullenly at a typewriter. A one-finger typist. Speed can't have been a consideration. The machine had no paper in it. She released the carriage, which shot back, toppling a vase of plastic flowers.

"Look," said Edmundo. "In that glass case by the door. A devil mask." It was hideous, intentionally grotesque. The head was horned, serpents rearing from the forehead and the eyes protruding as they would from a strangulation victim. It would be hard to imagine anything more ferocious.

"In the old days, before the Spanish came, the people who lived here were very devout," Edmundo explained. "They worshiped the sun. This made Huari, god of the underworld, very angry. He sent monsters to destroy them. You see the serpents on the mask? The monsters looked just like that."

"Did they succeed?"

"No, the people fought with great courage, and the monsters fled. This is the victory we celebrate when we do the devil dance at Carnival. The dancers wear masks just like that one."

"Is it wise to taunt the devil like that?"

"Oh, we don't really mean it," he said. "We're careful not to give offense."

At the table next to ours, two soldiers were having dinner. They were both very drunk, and we had just ordered coffee when the younger of the two leaped to his feet and grabbed his crotch. There was no doubting that his distress was genuine.

Wheeling first to the right and then to the left, he crouched a little as a look of terror crossed his face. "Jesus, Mary, and Joseph," he muttered. Little good it did him. A wet stain began to spread down the legs of his trousers, slowly at first and then more rapidly, until finally—he had now abandoned the struggle—rivulets of urine spilled over his shoes and edged across the floor. They were coming our way.

His agitated colleague, concerned as much for the reputation of the military as for his stricken friend, bowed low in our direction. "I would be grateful," he said, "if you mentioned this to no one."

Later, when the two had regained their composure, they invited us to their table for drinks. The one with the weak bladder was named Juan; the other was Ignacio.

"You have to stay for Carnival," said Juan when I mentioned I would be leaving the next morning.

"That's just what I've been saying," said Edmundo. It was growing dark, and the waiter had put a candle on the table. "He's never seen the devil dance."

"Never seen the devil dance?" said Juan. "He can't leave Oruro until he does."

He got to his feet. "I'll be back," he said.

He returned wearing the devil mask. It now looked a lot less fearsome. The urine stain still visible on his trousers may have explained it. Incontinence, even when it's satanic, rarely awes.

"Now watch," he said, barely audible through the plaster of paris. He swooped around the table waving his arms, the mask's elongated ears quivering, its glass teeth throwing back the candlelight. He whirled, steadied himself and sprang into the air—an astonishing feat for a man in his condition. He whirled and sprang again. But this time he landed badly and collided with the table. Several glasses crashed to the floor, and the coffeepot—its contents, thank goodness, no longer hot—fell into my lap. Now I too sported wet trousers.

"Well, what did you think?" he said, trying to struggle out of the bright red mask. It wouldn't budge. "Did you like it?"

"It was remarkable," I said, a little self-conscious about addressing that furious face and those goitrous eyes.

"The miners were taught the dance by Huari himself," said Ignacio. "A group of them fell asleep in a mine not far from here, and when they woke up, there was the devil. Dancing his heart out."

A shadow fell across the table. We had been joined by Ignacio's girlfriend, and she was clearly livid. So terrifying did she look that even Juan, still in his devil mask, quailed before her. She and Ignacio had arranged to see a film together—and he had forgotten about it.

"I thought I'd find you here, you ne'er-do-well," she bellowed. "A little drunk, are we? Escaping life's cares? You weasel! I've known more loyal rats." She went on to enumerate the humiliations he had made her suffer. Their life together had been one degradation after another, she said, indignity heaped on indignity and insult compounding insult. Why, he was hardly a man at all; he was a sniveling creature, and she was much too good for him.

Ignacio, to his credit, bore this with equanimity, even managing to fall asleep, which only inflamed her all the more. Reaching for a beer bottle, she brought it down hard on his head. He paid this no heed either, his snoring continuing uninterrupted.

She now turned on the devil. "Don't I know you from somewhere?" she asked the mask. "You're one of his no-good friends, right? It's because of you that he's drunk all the time. You worm."

Her blood up, her denunciations grew more shrill. She seemed not to notice that the devil was slipping lower and lower in his seat. Down, down he went until only his horns were visible. And then he slipped out of view altogether, landing with a crash on the floor. Drink had claimed another victim.

I met an anthropologist on the bus to Siglo Veinte.

"You can call me Dr. Browne," he said. It made me wonder what others were allowed to call him.

Normally, Dr. Browne lectured at one of England's less prestigious universities. For now he was on sabbatical in Potosí, studying a tribe of Indians who resented his attention.

"They're being very belligerent." He laughed. "They've threatened to kill me."

Did they mean it?

"They gave me to believe they did."

How do they kill?

"With axes." He giggled, at pains to appear a man who made light of difficulty. "They're proficient at it too, by all accounts. That's why I'm going to Siglo Veinte. Thought I'd lie low for a while. What are you doing here?"

"I'm visiting the mines. I have a letter of introduction to someone in Catavi."

"Take my advice and avoid Catavi," he said. "That's where the bosses live. The miners live in Siglo Veinte."

He sighed. "You'll like the miners," he went on. "A fine group. If there is one man to whom I feel myself inferior, it is a Bolivian tin miner. And I don't care who knows it."

"Orwell said the very same thing about the miners in the north of England," I said.

"Oh, I don't see very much to admire in them. They're a lot of atavists. Their conduct during the coal strike was disgraceful. The police were much too lenient. I'd have locked all of them up."

Incongruously, this man who denounced union violence in England complained that Bolivian unions were not being violent enough. "This country continues to be run by a small group of very privileged people, and the unions are doing nothing about it. It's shameful."

"What is it you propose they do?"

"Simple! Build socialism."

"I shouldn't think that's simple. But suppose it were: how should they go about it?"

"The only way: guerrilla warfare. I'd give the miners guns. They fought the army to a standstill once before. Why can't they do it again?"

"Well, for one thing, the army is now a lot more sophisticated. Remember, it made short work of Che."

"Think guerrilla warfare is dead, do you?" he asked. "You're wrong about that. Guerrilla warfare, alone, can liberate the people. It's men, not weapons, that make the difference. As international experience proves."

As I expected, he loathed the IRA. It kills innocent people, he said. They were innocent, I suppose, because some of them were English. Those who would die in Bolivia, if the miners ever took to arms, would represent some Other, and their deaths could be more easily countenanced. Distance makes the heart grow callous.

Catavi is flanked on two sides by tailings. These huge, inert dunes are its most dramatic feature, and from a distance they look like fortifications. But they provide no protection. Lacking function, they provide nothing. They are dead matter unable to sustain the roughest grass. Featureless and without color, their lifelessness repels. Even children, who might have been expected to use them for their sport, instinctively stay away.

Between the flanks of these dunes, a forklift truck had become mired, and I watched the laborious effort to extricate it. When digging failed, a tractor was dispatched. But it too became embedded. More digging, and then the rescue mission was abandoned.

It was an example of the steady attrition, the capacity ever dwindling, that afflicts this place. Attracting little investment, the mines are starved for capital. This is a dying industry, and everything about Catavi seemed crippled: the run-down cottages, the abandoned tractor, a limping boy—his right foot turned inward—and a one-legged man on crutches. Even the dogs appeared lame. Only the dunes flourished. I imagined them mounting higher and higher, while Catavi, beside them, dwindled to nothing.

"The bosses you spoke of seem not to be doing very well," I said to Dr. Browne, who had stifled his scruples and come to Catavi with me. Doing so, he said, would give him a chance to know the enemy.

"That's the tragedy," he said. "They have as much to gain from a socialist revolution as anyone, but they're implacably opposed to it."

I spotted two people I had seen on the bus—a couple in black. They had come to attend the funeral of a man who'd died of silicosis—or *mal de mina*, as the miners called it.

"I spoke to them in Oruro," said Dr. Browne. "They are relatives."

"They're looking a little lost."

"I expect they've been told to make themselves scarce. Until the dead are actually interred, they're believed to have the power to take other family members to the afterworld with them. That's why nonrelatives prepare the body for burial. It's supposed to reduce the risk."

"What is their afterworld like?"

"From what I can gather, it's just like this one."

"What? Tailings and stricken tractors and lame dogs?"

"But there's lots to eat and drink, apparently. For people who exist on potatoes, that's no small thing."

Silicosis is a miserable disease. Its victims are unable to discharge water and swell horribly, sometimes growing to twice their normal size. When the swelling abates, paralysis ensues. Conventional medicine is of little help, and many victims turn to herbal healers to relieve their suffering.

"The healers rub the body with a mixture of wine and alcohol," said Dr. Browne, "and prescribe a diet of broiled cat—the cat must be black—and vicuña blood. In one case I heard of, the healer killed a pair of lizards after walking them across the sick man's back. Supposedly, the lizards draw out the disease. It's transferred from him to them. When they die, the silicosis dies with them."

Walking back to Siglo Veinte, we stopped at the Campo de María Barzola. It was here, on December 21, 1942, that an army colonel ordered his soldiers to fire on striking miners.

It was the most fateful decision in recent Bolivian history; because of it Bolivia would be changed forever.

The unarmed miners were marching to Catavi to press for higher wages, and with them were their families—an estimated six thousand women and children. Ordered to turn back, they pressed on, the women and children now moving forward to take up positions at the head of the march. The intention, one said later, was to make it impossible for the army to shoot.

The army didn't scruple. At point-blank range, seven hundred soldiers armed with machine guns opened fire. Among the first to fall was María Barzola. The mining enclaves had seen other massacres—in 1919, 1922, and 1927—but this was by far the bloodiest. When the shooting stopped five hours later, some four hundred people had died.

In the inquiry that followed, the government would blame their deaths on Communist provocateurs. Later it would claim that Nazi agitators had been responsible. It had evidence, it said, that seamen from the *Graf Spee* had been in Catavi when the confrontation occurred. And it defended the army's action, saying that the miners were some of the best-paid workers in the country and that their strike had been illegal.

The Catavi massacre became a watershed. It galvanized the Bolivian left and intensified pressure for change. It resulted too in the miners founding a union that would quickly become the most powerful in the country, be decisive in bringing the MNR (the Movimiento Nacionalista Revolucionario) to power in 1952, and dictate both the character and the pace of the revolution that followed.

Bolivia's revolutionary era began in April 1952, when armed miners marched on La Paz and joined forces with civilians loyal to the MNR. Together they fought the army to a standstill, making it possible for the MNR to form a government with Víctor Paz Estenssoro as its leader. For a time the miners strongly influenced the new administration, setting its agenda and pushing it further and further to the left. Over the opposition of the MNR's more moderate elements, the bigger mines were nationalized, an agrarian-reform law was drafted, and, for the first time, Indians were allowed to vote.

Nationalization was to produce major dislocations. Exports plummeted, and by 1956 Bolivia was bankrupt. Realizing that the country lacked the resources to underwrite its own development, Paz Estenssoro, himself a moderate, yielded to U.S. pressure and announced a stabilization program. Bolivia would balance its budget, abolish food subsidies, hold down wages, cut government spending, and end labor's role in running the mines.

The power of the miners had now been broken, and they had no one to blame but themselves. By pressing their radical agenda on what was essentially a middle-class government, they had given Paz Estenssoro little choice. They had committed the great sin of Bolivian politics: they had pushed their demands long after it was expedient to do so. They had abused their power.

Before the miners could regroup, Paz Estenssoro began to resupply the army while cutting off arms to the worker militias. Once again, the army had the upper hand and, in 1964, Paz Estenssoro was deposed. The military had returned to politics after a twelve-year absence and would run Bolivia until the perennial Paz Estenssoro would again be elected president in 1985.

"It doesn't surprise me that the miners would be radical," said Dr. Browne. "They have been jailed, exiled, murdered—and all it has served to do is make them more conscious than ever of who they are and what is being done to them. They are now the only force in the country capable of seizing power in the name of the people."

In Siglo Veinte the next morning, I was entrusted to the care of Alfonso.

"You'll need protective clothing," he said. "Let's see what we can find."

A search lasting ten minutes turned up a pair of Wellingtons, an oilskin jacket, and a miner's helmet.

"Is this all?" I asked. I felt a little vulnerable.

"It's all anyone wears," he said.

"There's something wrong with this helmet. The lamp doesn't work."

"Here," he said, handing me a battery pack. "Hang this from your belt."

These lamps have an unexpected benefit. Because of them, you know immediately when you're being looked at. Just a glance in your direction, and a beam of light falls across your face.

Half a mile underground, Siglo Veinte is the biggest tin mine in the world, so vast that, although hundreds work here, one can travel great distances and rarely meet a soul. When one does—the lamp visible long before the miner is—it is usually one man working alone.

There seemed little group effort unless a hole was being drilled, in which case the miners worked in teams of two. One man held an aging pneumatic drill while the other directed the pin.

"Drilling is one of the worst jobs down here," said Alfonso. "The vibrations make you numb. I've had rocks fall on me and not felt them after a day's drilling."

We trudged everywhere, heads bent because of the low ceiling. In the darkness, and crouched like that—I noticed too that I was scuttling—I had the sensation for a moment of having become a cockroach.

Alfonso wandered into a tunnel to urinate. "Sorry," he

said, when he got back. "There are no toilets down here. No toilets and no water."

There are no facilities of any kind, and no refuge from the heat, which sometimes exceeds 100 degrees. The lunchroom was a low niche often filled with silicates.

Two figures ran down the tunnel toward us, their fingers in their ears. "Get down," said Alfonso, pulling me to my knees.

Then, *boom!* The shock wave tipped my helmet over my eyes. Alfonso grinned. "Dynamite," he said.

"Aren't you warned before they detonate that stuff?"

He laughed. "Why do you think so many of us are killed?"

Alfonso was forty-five, but he looked older.

"I'm one of the lucky ones," he said. "Many of us can't work after forty. Most people my age have disability pensions."

Was he healthy?

"I'm all right for the moment. But, of course, I'm contaminated."

What did he dream about?

"The darkness. And the noise. The hissing of the pistons, the dynamite exploding. Sometimes, it wakes me up."

Siglo Veinte is largely exhausted. Tin production has been falling since 1929—as has investment. Without new technology and a major effort to find new deposits, all the miners can do is scrape up what little tin is still accessible.

"The government refuses to give us money," said Alfonso. "Look at those supports. They should be replaced, but we have no wood. And you saw our first-aid station. No bandages, no antiseptics, nothing."

Because equipment is old and methods primitive, Bolivian tin sells for less than it costs to produce it. Lacking the money to modernize, the government has begun closing mines. Some seven thousand miners, out of a work force of thirty thousand, have lost their jobs in just twelve months. As an alternative to layoffs, the miners are being encouraged to move to Bolivia's eastern lowlands. So far, there have been few takers.

"For one thing," said Alfonso, "I don't think of those people in the lowlands as being Bolivians at all. We have nothing in common with them. They're another race. And what would I do there? Farm? What do I know about farming?"

He complained that people from the Altiplano can't survive at low altitudes. "I know people who have gone there and died," he said. "It's the air. It's different somehow."

"Yet stay in the mines, and you may die, too," I said. "You said so yourself."

"But here, I die among my own people."

Alfonso was more self-aware than Marco had been, his world larger. He wanted to know if I supported the British action in the Falklands. Did I like the queen? Was I middle class or working class? (The latter, he made it clear, was better.) What did meat cost in London? When would tin prices revive? Were English miners well paid? He was saddened to hear that in Britain too miners were feeling the pinch.

"But they can't be as bad off as we are," he said. "I earn forty dollars a month. Did you know that we're as poor today as we were a century ago? That's why we're socialists. That's why we'll always resist. The mining vanguard will never perish."

Alfonso took me to see the *tío*, the mine's presiding spirit. I recognized him immediately. Horned head, glass teeth, protruding eyes. It was the devil—Huari, god of the underworld. Three feet high and made of cement, he was painted a bright pink. Streamers had been placed around his shoulders, and his penis was fully erect. From these demonic loins, munificence was believed to flow—luck, progeny, wealth.

Representing the male principle, Huari, while he has his uses for women, doesn't much like them. This is why the miners invite their wives underground only once a year: on

December 21, Bolivia's Labor Day and the anniversary of the Catavi massacre. Although women were enlisted to mine tin when Bolivia fought Paraguay for control of the Chaco, their presence in the mines is generally regarded as tempting fate.

The miners think of the *tío* as owning the mine, and before beginning work they make him an offering. This is to stay on his good side—rather like an apple for the teacher. Coca leaves are placed in Huari's mouth, and the small canister he carries is filled with alcohol.

In the past, Alfonso said, this tradition would occasionally lapse, at which times the miners were invariably overtaken by tragedy. Accidents multiplied, and workers died. Alfonso himself credited these daily offerings with saving his life. A year earlier, he said, he had been struck by a falling rock. "If it weren't for the *tío*, it would have killed me."

In the absence of coca to eat, Alfonso explained, the *tío* ate miners. By contrast, if the miners took care of him, he took care of them.

"We honor him," he said, "and in return, the *tío* keeps us safe."

When the *tío* has been given coca, the miners roll quids of their own. They consume a lot of coca, the leaf from which the alkaloid cocaine is extracted: as much as 10 ounces each a week. The coca leaf is sold openly all across Bolivia—the law only prohibits using it to manufacture coke—and the miners buy theirs in the *pulperías* (general stores). Management is careful to keep them well supplied. "If we ever ran out of coca," one official told me, "we'd have a war on our hands."

Coca, for these men, has become a necessity. It gives them energy and blunts the appetite. Without it their jobs would be intolerable. Yet coca is becoming expensive, a consequence of international demand. According to Alfonso, many miners are finding it hard to afford.

The good Dr. Browne saw the practice of chewing coca as

no more significant that the English tea break. But there are differences. By reducing the appetite, coca makes the miner disinclined to eat, contributes to his undernourishment, and increases his chances of falling ill.

Alfonso and I went aboveground. It was a shock to be in the light again. The sun so dazzled that I was forced to cover my eyes. The world looked so clean. It gleamed, glowed, sparkled.

From the distance came the sound of rifle fire. "Soldiers," said Alfonso. "There's an army barracks a mile away. They stay in practice in case we ever strike."

Was he here in 1967?

"When the miners were massacred again? Yes."

He pointed. "You see those hills? There were army snipers there." He pointed again. "And over there. We were fired on from two sides. All we had was dynamite. We were no match for guns."

How many people died?

"Dozens. So many, the hospital hadn't room for them. There wasn't time to bury them. They were burned, instead."

He had been in the mine when the army moved in. Communications were cut, and their wives were unable to get word to them, but the miners had been expecting trouble. When their shift ended, they left the mine through a shaft on the other side of Siglo Veinte. The army was caught off guard. But not for long. The military advantage proved decisive.

"They fired on us for hours," said Alfonso. "All we could do was lie low and wait for them to stop.

"What a year that was. My wife was beaten by a soldier and lost her baby. And a few months later, my brother Augusto was killed. He'd gone to Santa Cruz to fight with Che."

It embarrasses the miners that more of them didn't rally to Che Guevara. Leftists in many parts of the world—Dr. Browne among them—have criticized them for it. Yet Che made no serious effort to mobilize the miners—one of many errors in his ill-conceived campaign.

"How old was your brother?"

"Nearly twenty-five. Che said the true revolutionary is guided by love. That was Augusto. He sent me a letter just before he died. I keep it in my wallet. Would you like to read it?"

"Very much."

"Wherever death may surprise us," I read, "it will be welcome provided that this, our battle cry, reaches some receptive ear; that another hand be extended to take up our weapons; and that other men come forward to intone our funeral dirge with the staccato of machine guns. Let Bolivia resound to our cry of Victory or Death!"

When I was leaving, Alfonso asked for my address.

"A very nice American was here last month," he said. "We are going to write to one another."

He showed me the address in his notebook. It was obviously fictitious: 99 Frog Lane, Tadpole, New England.

"A very nice young man," he said again.

I felt rather bad for him, but Alfonso, it turned out, was something of a fraud himself. In Catavi later an engineer asked if he and I had gotten along.

"We did, indeed," I said. "I liked him a lot. What a lot of tragedy he's had in his life."

The engineer smiled. "He told you about his brother?"

"The guerrilla? Yes."

"He tells that story to everyone who comes here. It's not true. Alfonso has no brother. Never did."

"But he showed me a letter from him."

"About death or victory? That's something of a joke around here. He transcribed it from a book. He doesn't mean any harm by it. It's just his little vanity."

5

THE TRIP to Potosí was enlivened by the presence on the bus of a drunk. After being carried to his seat, he fell asleep, then woke suddenly and vomited on everyone around him. Now much relieved, he fell asleep again, leaving it to his wife to make his apologies. She had only done so when he woke a second time and vomited once more. He spent the rest of the sixteen-hour journey with his head buried in her chest. A good-looking, smartly dressed woman, she stroked his head and made crooning noises. If he had humiliated her, she seemed not to mind.

Those on whom he had been sick were—not surprisingly—less forgiving. Still, it was unusual to hear criticism expressed at all. I had been on numerous Bolivian buses and seen many incivilities, but never before had I heard people grumble.

Perhaps because most bus travel in Bolivia is nocturnal, the normal courtesies are suspended. Under cover of darkness, people may imagine themselves anonymous, free—as at some masked ball—to commit their indiscretions without fear of discovery. Which is not to say that these indiscretions were particularly grave. They were more in the nature of peccadilloes—though no less vexing for that. When, for example, you shut a window—it is freezing cold—and it is promptly opened again, or when you open it because the heat is suffocating and it is instantly shut, it is hard not to imagine yourself just a little put upon. And when a man puts a sack of potatoes in your lap—"Just for a moment," he assures you—and then disappears, when a mother hands you a howling baby and falls asleep for three hours, or when a dog chews a hole in your shirtsleeve—"He likes you," says the owner— rare is the man who wouldn't feel a little cross.

Most of these impositions have their origins in the competition for space. It wouldn't matter so much that Bolivia's buses are old and ramshackle if they weren't also so very crowded. Not only are the seats filled but so are the aisles. And the stairwells too. Space is so scarce that people fight, not only to preserve what is theirs but to incorporate as much as possible of what is yours. Which is why those first few minutes as the bus fills are so critical. You wait anxiously to see who will sit beside you, and when he materializes—it is usually a he, women preferring to sit with women—you glare at each other like stags, antlers twitching.

Then he sits down, and the hostilities begin. First, as often as not, he will try to put a bag under your seat. Since this restricts your legroom, you resist vigorously, driving back the bag until it is under *his* seat. No words are spoken. By tradition, these contests are conducted silently. Then, in all likelihood, he will shift in his seat until, little by little, he occupies much of yours in addition to his own. Obviously, this cannot be tolerated. Force must be met with force. And immediately. Time is of the essence, because tolerate these incursions even for a minute and you are deemed to have waived your rights.

Not everyone fights with the same intensity. Some capitulate right away. Either they lack the temperament or experience has taught them that defeat is inevitable. Others skirmish for the length of the trip. In such cases there are no winners, the protagonists succumbing finally to mutual exhaustion. More commonly, though, a détente will be established. Yet even then you must maintain your guard. Relax your vigilance even for a moment, and before you know it that wretched mongrel is gnawing at your shirt again.

Now that the country has an air transit system, people of means fly when they travel within Bolivia. Those who can't afford air travel take the bus. Which is why it is not the custom on Bolivian buses to offer around—even by way of formality—one's food, one's drink, or one's reading material. Nor does one share one's blanket, something I had special reason to regret since I was traveling without one.

I had assumed people to think that since I didn't have a blanket I couldn't really need one, and that my remarks about ice forming on the windows were an attempt at conversation. Dr. Browne, who by coincidence was returning to Potosí on the same bus, took a different view. "As they see it, anyone traveling without a blanket at this altitude must be soft in the head," he said.

"And their compassion doesn't extend to nitwits?"

"Their generosity is not disinterested. They are kind to people who can be kind to them. You are a stranger. They have nothing to gain from being nice to you."

"And you, I would guess, find this commendably hardheaded."

"Well, I find much to admire in it," he said. "It's an example of Toynbee's challenge and response. People as poor as they are naturally regard demands on their resources with less than enthusiasm. For them, one's first duty is to fend for oneself. Self-sacrifice, because of the threat it poses to one's own survival, they regard as irresponsible."

"You're telling me to buy myself a blanket?"

"You would be more comfortable."

For the moment, though, I was not to go cold. There were two Australians on the bus—Paul and Kerry—and Kerry lent me his poncho. They had been in Bolivia a month, having come from Peru, where they had spent six weeks. They much preferred Bolivia.

"I had the shits the entire time I was in Peru," said Paul, "but here, I've been fine. Four weeks, and I haven't had the shits once."

"But I have wind," admitted Kerry. And in case I doubted it, he farted loudly—something he was to do repeatedly for the rest of the journey. To the rigors of bus travel, a new horror was added.

We stopped for supper. The men got out to piss, and the women bought sandwiches. I looked up quite casually, and the sky took my breath away. It was unbelievably beautiful. Because there wasn't a light for miles—nothing but this candlelit tea shop and a votive lamp burning at a shrine across the road—the stars were brighter than I had ever seen them. Densely packed, they were crammed more tightly than we on our miserable bus.

"Why is the southern sky so much more splendid?" I asked Paul, with whom I was sharing a cup of coffee.

"More splendid than what?" he said.

"The northern sky."

"Tilt, I think. It has something to do with the earth's tilt."

At a signal from the driver, people abandoned their half-eaten suppers and trooped back to the bus. Bus drivers have enormous moral authority in Bolivia. They enjoy something of the status of folk heroes. And with good reason, because without them—and their truck-driving counterparts—there would be little travel in this country. Trains are slow and unpredictable; flying is expensive and unpredictable; and private cars, knowing what's good for them, steer clear of Bolivia's primitive highways. In a country where geography has always hindered contact, the bus driver, it would not be too fanciful to say, is a modernizing force. By facilitating communication, he is helping to integrate the country, defuse regional rivalries, and foster a sense of national identity.

Still, I hardly think that this is why his passengers refer to him as *maestro*, give him presents of cigarettes and oranges, and compete to be allowed to sit beside him. Bus drivers are romantic figures, genial freebooters who affect the air of men who have learned to laugh at the world, men adequate to anything fate might hand them. In Bolivia that can be any number of things: mud slides, dead llamas, overturned trucks, and endless mechanical failures. On the trip to Potosí we broke down three times.

"Is it bad?" someone asked the driver as he peered into the engine.

"Very bad," came the answer.

And the word spread through the bus. "It's very bad. We may be here all night." Everyone looked hugely pleased. They relished this setback. It lent the trip an air of drama, added a touch of peril. Now we would be spared the embarrassment of arriving in Potosí on time.

The third breakdown seemed by far the most serious. The engine whined like a Cuisinart, coughed, and then fell silent. The driver held up something for our inspection: the gear stick. It had come away in his hand.

Again he went to work, the passengers watching more out of curiosity than out of anxiety. Again the word went around. "It's very bad. We could be here all night." But no one really believed it. We'd come to no harm. Didn't the driver know what he was doing? Indeed he did. An hour later the bus was pronounced roadworthy again, and we resumed our way. Now even I began to see him as something of a wizard.

He drove like a maniac. This man scorned danger, taking the narrow mountain road as if we were on some wall of death. The bus had an orange interior, and I had the sensation for a moment of being hurled to hell in a tangerine. Didn't this man have loved ones? Wouldn't he like to see his wife again?

Headlights in the distance. Another bus coming toward us. One of us would have to yield. On our right, a rock face. No quarter there. On our left, a fall of several hundred feet. Our driver picked up speed. He might have been a medieval knight, lowering his visor, gripping his lance, spurring on his steed. Inches separated the buses when they thundered past each other. The driver glanced back and winked. I may have been the only one to notice. Everyone else seemed fast asleep.

We reached Potosí shortly after dawn. We were now at an altitude of 13,000 feet, and the cold was vicious. It will warm up when the sun's been out a bit, I thought. But it didn't. It snowed instead.

Everyone looked frozen: the people bustling to work, their hands tucked in their armpits; the children on their way to school, snow glistening on their raven hair; the market women, faces glowing red, peering from deep within their kiosks; the policeman shadowboxing in an effort to keep his blood moving.

It seemed not at all "the place of evil enchantment" Joseph Andrews claimed to have found here 150 years ago. But Andrews may have been remembering Potosí's extraordinary past. In the sixteenth century it would indeed have seemed enchanted. Enchanted and very dangerous.

In 1545 there was discovered in Potosí—the mountain for which the city is named—the richest silver deposit anywhere, and for the next two centuries the imperial city flourished, becoming the biggest and richest in the Americas. By one estimate, Potosí was to yield 20,000 tons of silver. (Today silver in that quantity would fetch billions of dollars.) Its coat of arms referred to it as the "treasure of the world; the king of all mountains, and the envy of all kings." And as its fame spread, it became synonymous with huge wealth. The phrase *as rich as Potosí* became a byword around the world.

In Potosí, it was said, even the poor wore silk. Nearly everyone had money to spend, and in this *emporium mundi* one could buy anything one wanted. A writer of the time left this partial shopping list: Portuguese linens, French embroideries, Flemish tapestries, Dutch textiles, German swords, Florentine satin, English hats, Venetian glass, Indian ivory, Chinese porcelain, Angolan slaves, West Indian cocoa, Arabian perfumes, Persian carpets, and Ceylonese diamonds.

All Potosí lacked was news of the outside world. It didn't learn until April 1599 that King Felipe II had died the previous September. (It made amends by offering thousands of masses for the dead king's soul.) And seven months elapsed before it heard that Felipe's successor had taken a queen— Princess Margarita of Austria. But Potosí didn't need news. It prospered anyway, tales of its wealth becoming legend. Stories were told of beggars who dined off silver plate at the homes of the well-to-do, and brides whose dowries relieved their husbands of ever having to work again. One man reputedly paid a fortune for a trout.

Most profligate of all was the mine owner José de Quiroz. In his home Quiroz kept a large chest, and every evening the poor were invited to select one of its many drawers, the contents of which they might then keep. Some of these drawers were empty; others contained thousands of dollars. Quiroz's most enduring legacy may be "Let's Make a Deal."

With its promise of easy pickings, the city attracted droves of fortune seekers—not always the most scrupulous of people. Potosí became virtually lawless. Nowhere was life more tenuous. To avoid being killed, people wore chain mail and took fencing lessons. Men battled one another in the streets—

over mining claims, gambling debts, women. Especially
women, who, being in short supply, were ever in contention.
In an effort to restore the peace, the Crown threatened to
repatriate men whose wives were still in Spain.

Even the clergy bore arms—and didn't hesitate to use them.
Usually on one another. Religious processions were a special
source of friction. Jealous of their prestige, rival orders com-
peted for the best positions. Would the Jesuits precede the
Franciscans, or the Franciscans the Jesuits? And what of the
Benedictines? And the Dominicans? Surely they were not
expected to bring up the rear?

Potosí adored processions, expending on them the same
energy and love of excess that characterized its other activ-
ities. One of the more extravagant occurred in 1687. Fearing
an earthquake, the city decided it should atone. The historian
Bartolomé Arzáns de Orsúa y Vela described the scene:

> [Men with] covered faces [performed] harsh and bi-
> zarre acts of penitence: some lashing themselves with
> savage whips; others wounding themselves with metal-
> tipped scourges; some whose bodies were tightly wrapped
> in ropes of straw and bristle; many dragging terribly
> heavy chains, barefoot, and lashing themselves cruelly;
> others with their arms extended in the form of a cross
> and tied to a heavy beam borne on the nape of their
> necks; and others walking with their hands tied behind
> their backs, gags in their mouths, and prickly haircloth
> on their bodies, with ropes around their necks pulled by
> Negroes and other low people.

Children marched too, most of them naked, with the not
surprising result that many fell ill "and four of the more
sickly died."

Sustaining all this extravagance, all this indulgence was

the *mita*, the system of compulsory Indian labor instituted in 1570 and abolished by Simón Bolívar only in 1825. "It was slavery," said José, an old man I met in the market one afternoon. Despite the cold, he and a number of others were waiting in line for a *prognóstico cardíaco*, first weighing themselves on a bathroom scale and then completing a questionnaire. He asked to borrow my pen. "Are you excitable?" one question asked. "Have your feet ever turned blue?" inquired another. When he'd finished, we found a bar and had a drink.

"The *mitayos*," said José, "worked one week in every three and one year in every seven. That was the theory. But they were paid practically nothing, and they borrowed to support themselves. That was the trap. You can borrow a lot in twelve months. So they had to stay on when their year ended—to pay their debts. This they never did because, to survive, they had to keep on borrowing.

"If they didn't borrow, they didn't eat," said this man, once a miner himself, now a tailor. "Their families were expected to feed them, but it was all a family could do to feed itself. And as often as not, the *mitayo*'s wife and children worked with him. It was the only way he could meet his quota— which got bigger and bigger and bigger. If he fell short, he was flogged. Many *mitayos* were flogged to death."

Others developed pneumoconiosis—the first occupational disease diagnosed in the Americas. Still others died of exhaustion. They were buried where they fell, their co-workers piling rubble on their bodies. Production continued uninterrupted.

The mortality rate has been estimated at 80 percent, but a precise death count may never be known. The record is vague. While some historians say the *mita* claimed 3 million lives, General William Miller, Potosí's English-born prefect in 1825, put the figure at 8 million.

A summons to work in the mines became something to

dread, and, since force was unavailable to them, the Indians responded the only way they could. Those eligible for the *mita*—men between the ages of eighteen and fifty—moved as far from Potosí as they could. They took their families with them. Whole villages emptied. By 1750 Potosí's environs were deserted.

But by then Potosí, most of its silver extracted, was on the skids. When Bolivia gained its independence, the city's population—160,000 in 1650—had dropped below 9,000. Today 100,000 people live here, and the king of all mountains—now disgorging tin—still provides them with a living. But soon the tin too will have gone.

Yet Potosí remains a potent national symbol. Visiting it, I felt I understood Bolivia a little better. Here, more than anywhere else, Bolivia's character was set. Potosí established a tone for all that was to follow, and even today—three centuries later—its buccaneering ways and its belief that a man who can defend himself might do anything he pleases provide a compelling example.

Bolivians regard the Potosí era not as a historic aberration but as something of a golden age. Part of its attraction is the example it offers of easy riches waiting to be pillaged. Many have convinced themselves that another Potosí is out there somewhere—ready to revive Bolivia's fortunes, ready to make it the envy of kings all over again.

"There's little to see in Potosí anymore," said José, sounding like Edmundo in Oruro. "We are bankrupt. No money, no ideas. But, thank God, we still have our beautiful women. Don't you find them lovely?"

I was unable to say. The weather being bad, very few had shown themselves. Those I had seen had so insulated themselves against the cold that their beauty could only be a matter of conjecture.

I was disappointed. Edmond Temple, an Englishman who

visited Potosí in 1826, had spoken highly of its women. Although he hesitated to compare them with their English counterparts—"the most beautiful in the world"—many were, he
said, "very finely formed." He particularly liked their ample
necks, by which he meant, he explained, "that part of the
person which ladies blushingly term bosom."

"When does it start to get warm?" I asked José. "Perhaps
I can stay until it does."

I don't recall his answer because just then Dr. Browne
entered the bar. No ordinary Dr. Browne. This Dr. Browne
was disheveled, flustered. And his nose was bloodied.

"What a relief to see you," he said when I called to him.
He was out of breath. "Do you think you could order me a
brandy? I need a minute to collect myself."

"What happened to you?"

"Those wretched Indians I'm studying. They come into
town occasionally. One of them must have recognized me. I
was jumped."

"Are you hurt?"

"I don't think so. Actually, my strength may have surprised
him. He ran off. But not before he punched me in the face.
Damn the man."

He patted his nose. It was bleeding again. This was too
much for José. Claiming to have work to do, he took his leave.

"Those people mean you no good," I said. "Maybe you
should study someone else."

"Oh, I can't do that. Though I will agree: They're an odd
lot. As are most of the Indians around here."

He knew of one community, he said, which separated its
llamas every spring, the males going in one pen, the females
in another. "Then they play to them on those reed instru-
ments of theirs. For days and days. Get the llamas really
agitated. And then they release them."

"And?"

"They rut."

"The llamas or the Indians?"

"The llamas. But afterwards, the women take off across the fields, and the men give chase."

"More rutting?"

"I believe so, though I've never actually seen it. Not the sort of thing I'd want to see, to be frank." He shuddered.

More curious still was the *tinku*—a simulation of the ancient clan wars enacted not far from here, in Macha.

"Two communities are involved," said Dr. Browne. "They've hated one another for as long as anyone can remember. No one knows why anymore. Anyway, once a year, each puts up its best fighter, and they slug it out.

"It's incredible. They look like crazed bikers. Leather helmets and breastplates. Even their arms are covered. And they wear leather gloves with brass knuckles. It's made to look like a sporting event, but it's really very vicious. As often as not, they fight to the death."

"And no one tries to stop them?"

"On the contrary. Death means a good harvest. They're encouraged to kill one another. And when it's over, everyone gets very drunk, and there's a free-for-all."

"Just like a medieval tournament. Each community represented by a champion, the armor, the hand-to-hand combat. . . ."

"In the tournament death was accidental. Here, the intention is to murder one another."

"Then why isn't something done about it?"

"No one dares. These are not people you'd want to antagonize." He sighed. "Maybe I *should* call it quits. Right now, I'd give anything to be home watching golf on the telly."

He raised a hand to his nose. It had begun to swell. "I've had enough of Potosí," he said.

Dr. Browne wasn't the first Briton to express that sentiment. At one time Potosí boasted an English population of several hundred. Mining engineers and their families, most of them hated it here. Few places less resemble England: no glimmering weirs, no sad moors, no lilac'd lanes. They tried to make it as much like home as they could. They had their own church, and their own school, and they lived in houses modeled on the Cotswold cottage. They even had their own graveyard. Death meant assimilation with a country whose ways they had resisted assiduously, but at least they were still together.

I was anxious to find this graveyard. I was in a mood to be moved. I imagined it being like the English cemetery Evelyn Waugh had found on Gibraltar, the graves "a pretty, Wedgwood pattern, with urns and delicate carved plaques." But the women in the tourist booth affected no knowledge of it.

One said she had never heard mention of an English graveyard. A second was more emphatic: Not only was there not now an English cemetery but there never had been one. And a third demanded to know how I had come to hear of such a place, and why, in any event, I would want to see it.

Intrigued, I went to the university and inquired. "I'm afraid I have bad news," said a woman in the library. She watched me closely as she spoke. "The graveyard is no more."

"It has passed on?"

"Many years back, it was destroyed. By a flood."

In Potosí floods were a constant danger. To provide the huge quantities of water needed by the mines, the Spanish had constructed reservoirs, which were always bursting.

I felt suddenly weak.

"You must excuse me," I said, "but I have to sit down."

"I understand," she said, guiding me to a chair. "This must be a great shock."

But I wasn't thinking of those obliterated graves. Altitude sickness—*mal de altura*—had struck. My head pounded, and my stomach turned. I tried to stand—and couldn't. All my energy had gone.

"You should be in bed," she said. "I'll get you a taxi."

Altitude sickness is another reason people avoid Bolivia. Almost everyone who comes here experiences some discomfort. And although its effects are usually temporary, in extreme cases people become so ill they have to leave the country.

People bred on the Altiplano experience similar symptoms at low altitudes—something that hasn't always been understood. In colonial times Aymara soldiers sent to the lowlands gained a reputation for cowardice because they seemed disinclined to fight. Only later was their lassitude explained medically. At the time it was thought that geography couldn't be a factor because Spanish soldiers fought with vigor, and they, after all, had come all the way from Europe.

I was feeling somewhat better by the time I got back to my hotel. Toad Hall, I called it, because the proprietor was known to her staff as the Frog. Unkind, but not unfair—the good lady was far from handsome.

Loyal to the superstitions of her forebears, the Frog lived in a constant state of terror, imagining herself beset by witches and evil spirits. Prepared to believe anything as long as it was bizarre, she sat in the hotel's tiny courtyard every afternoon with her shawl drawn tightly around her head, only her eyes visible. It was her neck that gave her the most concern, she said. A bare neck was an open invitation to vampires.

"They'll get me eventually," she said, "but I have no intention of making it easy for them."

"Why don't you stay indoors?" I suggested. "Perhaps you'd feel safer."

"What? And let them know I'm afraid? If they thought that, I'd never have any peace."

When I told her of the attack on Dr. Browne, she wanted to know if he had taken the precaution of drinking his assailant's blood.

"I'm afraid there wasn't time," I said. "The man punched him in the nose and then took off."

She shook her head. "I don't give much for his chances," she said with obvious satisfaction. Because of his oversight, she explained, Dr. Browne was now vulnerable to his attacker's spells.

The air is thick with spells, she said. One can't avoid them. Take her boyfriend. (I was surprised to learn she had one.) He had designs on her sister. But did she blame him? Not at all. Doubtless one of her enemies had enchanted him.

"Why?"

"To punish me. Why else?"

The Frog's superstitions almost proved my end. Because the netherworld unleashes its forces at nine every night, closing time was a prompt half past eight. One evening José and I met in his shop for a cup of coffee, and I got back to Toad Hall fifteen minutes late. I knocked and shouted to no purpose. The hotel was dead to the world.

I had only myself to blame. The tailor had suggested showing me the house in which the Twelve Apostles met the Blessed Souls. It was some distance off my route, but I went anyway. I was familiar with the story. Arzáns included it in his history.

In 1657 Potosí was in another of its panics, this one occasioned by thugs who roamed the city after dark, breaking into houses and raping their female occupants. They called themselves the Apostles, and they gained their entry by dressing one of their number as a woman. This was Magdalene, who would run to the front door and plead to be admitted because her husband was trying to kill her.

One night the Apostles chose as their target the home of two young sisters who prayed several hours a day for the souls in Purgatory. When their assailants burst in on them, the sisters, in a state of some dread, called on the souls for help. That their appeal was answered there can be no doubt because, moments later, the Apostles were seen to flee the house in terror.

In their haste they dropped their purses, which were found to contain a quantity of silver. By right this wealth was now the property of the young maidens, and they disposed of it in the only way appropriate: they offered masses for the souls who had been their saviors.

I hammered on the door of Toad Hall again. No one stirred. It began to snow. I'd better go back to José's, I was thinking, when a scream rent the night.

It sounded—although I had no way of knowing this—like the disembodied vampires the Frog had warned about. There was a second scream, followed by a third. Was the Frog meeting the end she had always predicted for herself? Had her time come as she always said it would?

Lights began going on in the hotel. More screams, this time from the hall. Sounds of a struggle. A man shouted. Then the door was pulled open, and the Frog's sister ran past me. She looked terrified. With good reason. Hot on her heels was the Frog, puffed up with rage and looking more fearsome than I had ever seen her. A woman with murder in her heart!

I learned later that the Frog had caught her boyfriend and her sister in flagrante. Reprehensible indeed, but I couldn't help feeling grateful. If they hadn't abandoned themselves to lust, I'd now be dead of frostbite.

6

To my enormous relief, Sucre was hot. Gloriously hot. I'd had enough of the Altiplano's icy horrors. For two months, I had done little but battle searing cold. In Potosí, I'd thought of nothing else. The struggle to stay warm consumed me, reducing me to an animal existence.

I lost all interest in the world. My concern now extended no farther than my own frame. Although it hardly seemed my frame anymore. I had shriveled. I walked with knees bent and shoulders pushed so high that my neck had disappeared. Everything about me looked centripetal. I might have been trying to swallow myself.

I washed infrequently—the water was never warmer than freezing—and slept in my clothes. I stopped reading—it was too cold to hold a book—and shunned company. I no longer cared to talk to anyone, not even the innocuous Dr. Browne. Who could think of talking when his marrow had turned to ice?

The language of rage makes frequent reference to heat. People breathe fire and blow their tops. Their blood boils, or they become inflamed. They get hot under the collar. Hoping to raise my temperature, I pondered old injuries—the indignities I had been made to suffer, the lies I had been told, the love withheld for no reason. I pondered them with equanimity. The cold made it impossible to care.

Since Toad Hall wasn't heated, I spent much of my time in bed. It was the only place I could be moderately comfortable. I ransacked the room's other cot and slept between two mattresses. I dreamed of the tropics: lush jungle and howling monkeys and sweltering heat, palm trees and hibiscus and fish leaping in warm streams, cockatoos and mangoes and sun. Lots of sun. Sun melting the ice caps. Sun making the oceans boil. Sun reducing the world to cinder.

When an errand forced me out, I would wrap myself in newspaper. I imagined it providing insulation. But its only effect was to stain my skin with printer's ink. Anyone chancing to see my back after one of these excursions could read there the morning's headlines.

And after all that misery, Sucre. So jolly, warm, bright, and happy. Almost Mediterranean in spirit. In appearance too. Much of the city is painted white—to enhance its colonial character. The effect is pagan, nearly. A sun-filled world in which people stroll in shirtsleeves and laugh a lot. Coloratura laughter, thrilling to hear. Full of runs and trills, agile, florid.

People rarely laughed in Potosí, it struck me now. Though no climatic determinist, I was prepared to believe the claim of Hippocrates that the climate of a place shapes the personality of its inhabitants. Whereas in Potosí people had seemed taciturn and reserved, those in Sucre had an amplitude about them, a vigor. I was quite sure I was going to like them.

The heat had a tonic effect. I could feel the life quickening in me. My shoulders receded, and my neck reappeared. I shed my second layer of clothing and ventured out-of-doors. I had my hair cut and my shoes polished. I bought a book, and once again talked to people. I had thawed.

Although Sucre is nominally Bolivia's capital, it is in La

Paz that congress convenes, and in La Paz too that the president resides. Sucre could dominate public life only as long as its silver miners set the national agenda. When silver prices collapsed at the turn of the century, power shifted to the tin magnates farther north.

Before 1900 congress met thirty-one times in Sucre, nineteen times in La Paz. Since then it has met only in the latter. Sucre, a major agricultural center, resents this diminution and speaks contemptuously of its rival as "that Indian city." It does, though, retain one branch of government, the Supreme Court, which at the time of my visit was trying the deposed dictator Luis García Meza.

To all appearances the government was determined that nothing disrupt the trial. The area around the Palace of Justice was closed to traffic, and soldiers armed with teargas launchers patrolled the perimeter. A curious precaution when you consider that the trial had ground to a halt a month earlier because nine of the court's twelve judges had removed themselves from the case. They were prompted to do so when a colleague narrowly survived an attempt on his life. No one doubted who was behind the attack. García Meza was still supported by sections of the army and was believed to have emerged from hiding to face the charges against him only after being assured that the trial would not be allowed to proceed.

García Meza was accused of murder, sedition, and armed revolt. His 1980 coup, Bolivia's most brutal, brought to power the so-called cocaine government. It was financed by drug smugglers—two of whom were given cabinet posts.

Although the drug lords could point to numerous members of congress their money had elected, this was the first time they had attempted anything so ambitious as installing their own government. Having done so once, there are real fears they may do so again. Unless, that is, García Meza is brought to justice. But this is something few expect to happen.

A teacher I spoke to referred to the stalled trial as an example of *falta de sanciones*—the immunity that people of García Meza's ilk enjoy in this country. "People like him do exactly as they please," he said. "They always have."

"And the public doesn't mind?" I asked.

"It might—if this weren't something it has come to expect. You have to understand that many Bolivians admire García Meza. It doesn't matter that he behaved excessively. For them, he is a man who won't submit to the general will. We respect people like that.

"What did he do? Plunder the country? That's what our leaders have always done. We would think it odd if they didn't. Politics here is a competition for spoils. An unpleasant reality, perhaps, but one we have learned to live with."

Didn't it matter that García Meza had placed himself above the law?

"That's something else our leaders have always done. Bolívar, our first president, placed himself above the law, and everyone since has followed his example. It has become the Bolivian way."

Then were García Meza not to go to jail, the teacher wouldn't mind?

"You don't change a culture by sending one man to prison."

From what I could gather, much of Sucre agreed with him. There were no marches demanding García Meza's incarceration, no mass demonstrations. The only people to venture near the Palace of Justice were the lovers lolling around a replica of the Eiffel Tower in the park across the street. It was rather depressing.

I did see one protest. Forty angry students swept through the plaza one afternoon. Several of them raised fists; others bore banners demanding justice. But it was not to the Supreme Court they were headed. Their destination was the university, and they were protesting not the abuse of executive power but the outcome of a student election.

No one in the plaza paid them any heed. A young army officer had seized their attention. He was wearing full military dress—white gloves, gold epaulets, a saber—and looked quite splendid. As he knew, of course. On the pretense of taking the air, he had come here to offer himself for our delectation. He traversed the plaza several times, walking like a model on a runway—lots of abrupt halts and sudden pirouettes. We especially enjoyed the pirouettes. They showed his sabor to good effect. Once, for variety, he stooped to smell a rose. Holding it to his face, he inhaled deeply and shut his eyes. A man intoxicated.

It was a masterly performance, and it ended only when a pigeon strayed too near. But by then the officer had tired of us anyway and, hailing a taxi, he departed our lives forever. Though not immediately. The taxi was unable to go anywhere because a funeral party blocked its path. And the funeral party was prevented from moving because its way was barred by a garbage truck. The taxi driver shouted at the mourners—most of whom were nuns—and the mourners shouted at the garbageman, who opened a newspaper and affected not to hear them. Driver and nuns intensified their clamor, and the garbageman looked more deeply involved than ever in his reading. On his pedestal above them, Antonio Sucre extended a conciliatory hand over the city named in his honor.

While I was out, my hotel room was broken into and my shaving kit taken. It was no great loss, but the *dueña* was beside herself. "To think this could happen in my own home," she moaned happily. "Isn't anywhere safe anymore?"

She was a woman of spectacular roundness. Her clothes,

much too small for a person of her size, had to strain to encompass her—seams stretching to the breaking point, buttons hanging on by a single thread. I never saw her wear anything but black. Her husband had died some ten years earlier, and she still grieved for him, she said. "Strange, isn't it? I never thought I'd miss him. But there you are. We never know when we're well off." She wrung her hands—things of such fleshiness she appeared to have no fingers.

A woman haunted by the whims of chance, she believed herself to live in a world in which the presiding force was a rolled newspaper trouncing people for the sport of it. Misfortune could overtake her at any moment, she was convinced. Even so, it was clear that a larceny under her own roof exceeded her wildest imaginings. The world was more dangerous than she had thought; she was even more imperiled. And there was the additional fillip that the object stolen had belonged not to her but to someone else.

"The world is in moral ruin," she said gleefully. "One of these nights, we'll be murdered in our beds. Imagine: Every one of us with our throats cut."

I was glad I had been able to make her happy. And at such small cost. The shaving kit was unimportant. Everything in it could be replaced. It was a present to whomever had taken it. Thank you whoever you are for leaving me the brush. That was kind. Did you know it was a gift? The shaving cream, by the way, is concentrated. Use just a little at a time.

The hotel was spotless. The *dueña* scrubbed it—all three uneven floors, all fifteen white-walled rooms—from stem to stern at least twice a week. Concern about the afterlife made her do it, she explained. "When I'm called before my maker— and it could happen at any moment—I don't want a dirty house on my conscience."

To make her cleaning easier, she had placed a ban on pictures and curtains. ("They collect dirt.") And furniture was kept to minimum. My room had a bed and a night table. Nothing else. The lobby was completely bare. The small courtyard was equally austere, every plant and blade of grass uprooted because "they only make a mess."

Gabriel, the *dueña*'s twenty-five-year-old nephew, lent me a razor. "Until you can buy one," he said. An economics student, he gave me to believe when I met him that he was a journalist. He even hinted that he represented several major papers in North America.

Our first conversation consisted of his showing off his knowledge of the kings and queens of England.

"Elizabeth, right? There's an Elizabeth. And a Henry. One at least. Maybe more. Eight? Really? If I were king, I wouldn't want a name anyone else had had. And then there's that one who burned the cakes. I've always liked him. What was he called?"

We went and had a drink together. After three beers Gabriel revealed a regrettable desire to please. Having succeeded in discerning my prejudices, he proceeded to cater to them for the rest of the evening.

"You admire the Indians? Ah, if only the Indians ran this country. Bolivia wouldn't be backward very long, believe me."

"You are a socialist? What this country needs is a major overhaul. We have to make a fresh start, forge new institutions. The old ways don't work."

"You like the Americans? Russia has nothing to teach us. It means the Third World only harm."

He got up to buy another round of drinks, jingling as he did so. He carried his keys clipped to the waist of his trousers. Evidence of having access to something, I supposed. Though to judge from their size, the access was to nothing more substantial than a front door and a briefcase. Many Bolivians wear their keys like this, but why left me at a loss. Gabriel claimed to wear his as he did to protect his clothes. But since he rarely wore anything grander than jeans, this was hardly plausible. I could only imagine that the Elizabethan key-penis metaphor explained the practice—that a bunch of keys had the same symbolic value as a codpiece.

Walking through the plaza on the way home, we chanced on María, one of Gabriel's girlfriends. She had a clubfoot, something that clearly embarrassed him. "I like her very much," he told me later, "but she is like a sister to me. Nothing more."

He tried to borrow money from this woman, but she was not in a mood to be generous and in the end would consent only to buy him an ice cream. The vendor was a young Indian—one of many in the plaza. They amused themselves by stealing one another's hats. The horns they used to alert prospective customers sounded like sea gulls.

Determined to make amends for the loss of my shaving kit, the *dueña* became solicitous for my safety. There were two kinds of people in Sucre, she said—thieves and murderers, and since there was little choice between them, I should avoid both. Determined that I come to no new harm while in her custody, she took to locking me in my room at night. The street door was kept locked at all times, and she refused to give me a key. It might fall into the wrong hands, she said. Instead I was provided with a coded knock, which changed once a week "for security reasons."

I was also given a list of food items that were to be avoided at all costs. (New items were added daily.) One after another, whole sections of the city were placed off-limits. There were banks to avoid because they were clearinghouses for drug money, pharmacists to steer clear of because they belonged behind bars, restaurants to shun because "the things they put in their *salteñas* would shame a Christian."

At breakfast one morning, she came to my table and said it was her one consolation that the embassy knew of my whereabouts.

"What embassy?" I said.

She turned pale and crossed herself. "Jesus, Mary, and Joseph," she said. "Are you saying you haven't told your embassy you're here?"

"It never occurred to me. Is it really necessary?"

"Necessary? Do you know how many people come to Bolivia and are never heard of again? Suppose you disappeared? Forever!"

She seemed to be making a distinction between people who went somewhere and weren't seen again—they hadn't ceased to exist—and those who vanished off the face of the earth. One moment they were here; the next, they hadn't merely gone: they were nowhere. A phenomenon like spontaneous combustion. Although to combust—spontaneously or even after due deliberation—is not to disappear completely. One would be survived by one's teeth and one's shirt buttons.

The *dueña* seemed determined to infect me with her paranoia, and it made a rebel of me. I had lunch in the market—something she had expressly warned against—and from there I went to an ice-cream parlor also on her list of proscribed places. I'll show her, I thought. I had a banana split, an éclair, and a cappuccino—and felt sicker than I had in months.

Seated near me were four teenage girls, one of whom—she was quite ravishing—drew the attention of an aging gigolo. After several minutes of gazing on her like Cyrano on Roxanne, he sent a parfait to her table. A large wafer protruded from the top. At the sight of it, she and her friends collapsed in helpless giggles. Cyrano looked stricken. His nose was out of joint.

I walked to the university, where I had arranged to meet

Gabriel. I found him trading insults with another student, a little man with a glass eye. They had drawn a crowd. Both Gabriel and his opponent seemed a little drunk, and the exchange grew in acrimony. And then the man with the glass eye peeled off his jacket and hurled it to the floor. Gabriel looked taken aback, but he recovered himself and peeled off *his* jacket.

The man with the glass eye bristled and threw off his shirt. Gabriel bristled and followed suit. But he must have wished he hadn't. He was now looking a little frightened. His opponent too had begun to look desperate. The preliminaries had been exhausted. It was time to fight. But they continued to stall: Gabriel emptying his pockets and tying his shoelace, his opponent removing his hearing aid and asking someone to hold his watch.

And then, to the obvious relief of both, their friends intervened. Soothing, mollifying.

"There, there . . ."

"No, he didn't say that at all."

"You misunderstood him."

"That wasn't what he meant."

"You're too sensitive."

After a decent interval the two belligerents agreed that the offense, if there were any, had been unintended, and they embraced. The gallery burst into applause.

The whole thing had been preposterous, and, for fear of embarrassing him, I resolved not to mention it. It was he who brought it up. "Did you see that?" he wanted to know.

"What was it about?"

"The envy of the incomplete creature for a man brave enough to speak his mind," he said. "Offending people is the price I pay for being honest." This was surprising from a person who had lied about being a journalist.

"Have you seen the Virgin?" he asked suddenly. "You haven't? Then it's time you did."

The Virgin of Guadalupe is one of the richest statues in the world. It is two-dimensional—a flat piece of gold and platinum elaborately jeweled. Less than 2 feet high, it is triangular in shape, the flaring body topped by a tiny head. It reminded me of a flounder, and I might have laughed but for the Indian woman kneeling before it. Tears coursed down her face.

For all the statue's wealth, there is something pinched and parsimonious about it. Its rubies and emeralds are lackluster, and the eyes that gaze out at one lack expression. If they suggest anything at all, it is indifference. This is no celebration of faith. It is cold and modern and agnostic. By comparison, the other statues here, with their moonstruck expressions and eyes heavy with piety, seemed suddenly palatable.

The Virgin is revered in Bolivia. For the Indian, she is a manifestation of the Earth Mother; for the Hispanic, a lobbyist. Connections matter more than merit in this country, so it is understandable that people would hesitate to rely on virtue alone to secure their salvation. Hence the importance attached to the Virgin's intercessional powers. Who, after all, is better connected than she?

I found the statue impossible to admire. Both it and the Baroque altar on which it stands are too ornate. All that clamor has something febrile about it, and it made me wonder if the artist could have been quite right in the head. And yet it is typical of things here. There is an exaggeration, something forced about every aspect of life in this country. The laughter is too hearty, the courtesies too elaborate, the passion too inflammatory. Nothing is quite real. Bolivians love the preposterous.

An organ struck up. The playing was less than skillful,

but Gabriel was enchanted. "Listen," he said, seizing my arm. "Such feeling!"

And that is the crux of the matter. If you have feeling, you don't have to be good. Feeling is the crucial value. "Europeans have no feelings," he had once complained. He saw the northern existence as arid and desiccated. Bolivia was different. In Bolivia, he said, "we have life." Here one can't feel too much. The man who feels is more to be admired than the man who thinks. And the man who feels keenly is more admired still.

But it isn't enough to feel. Others have to know you feel. Which may explain why so many of the Bolivians I met claimed to be poets. Politicians, army officers, shop assistants—all wrote poetry, they said. Gabriel too. Gabriel wrote not just poetry but short stories and plays as well.

In his stories, people lie in bed and rail against Fate. "I am a victim of forces beyond my control," his characters are fond of saying. A surprising number of them die of asphyxiation. "That's how a lot of Bolivians feel," he explained. "Here we are in the middle of this big continent, cut off from everyone, and choking to death."

Gabriel's work in progress was a play about Mariano Melgarejo and the War of the Pacific.

"Don't contemporary subjects appeal to you?"

"This *is* a contemporary subject."

"But the war was fought a hundred years ago."

"Yes, but it isn't over. It won't be over until Bolivia regains Antofagasta."

Short of Chile returning that Pacific port—something it is not likely to do—there seems little chance Bolivia ever will regain it. Nonetheless the subject is discussed compulsively. Shops display decals demanding Antofagasta's reintegration, and the country maintains a small navy—in anticipation of Bolivia's again becoming a maritime nation.

Here past and present are easy to confuse—largely for the reason that the past, ever being revised, is no less kinetic than the present. Although Bolivia has some excellent historians, too much of its historiography consists of name-calling—a scholarship of calumny. It is said that only in Bolivia can one get up in the morning a simple private and go to bed a president. It is no less true that one can rise a president and retire an outcast. The search for whipping boys is relentless, and everyone is discredited eventually.

If history makes men wise, an absence of history—or in this case a false, tendentious one—produces idiocy. Bolivia is a country in the dark. A society without a true tradition of its own past, it has no clear idea of what it is or to what it aspires.

It is the fault of their history that Bolivians retain their fondness for scapegoats. It is always someone else who has engineered the country's difficulties. The middle class blames the aristocracy, the aristocracy blames the Indians, and everyone blames the politicians. Nowhere are politicians more widely reviled. "They are all thieves," you will be told. And the honest ones only appear so because their perfidies have still to come to light. Poor Bolívar. Is it any wonder he denounced this country?

Driven out of Caracas by royalist forces in 1815, Simón Bolívar fled to Jamaica. He returned to South America three years later, raised an army, and promptly liberated Colombia and Venezuela. By 1822 he had freed Ecuador. Two years later it was the turn of Peru. Yet for all his achievement Bolívar too was defamed for a time. The most powerful figure in South America in 1825, he died five years later penniless and forgotten. He was buried in a borrowed shirt. His will provided that the University of Caracas receive his library: a copy of Rousseau's *Social Contract* and a book on military tactics once owned by Napoleon. And to Bolivia he bequeathed the gold medal that country had bestowed on him when it named him its Protector.

This was an extraordinary reversal for a man whose name had so recently resounded around a continent—the Father of Bolivia, President of Colombia, Supreme Chief of Peru. In Sucre he had even inspired a hymn:

> All that is good
> Comes from you, Lord
> You gave us Bolívar
> Glory be to thee, great God.

I began to feel some sympathy for this strange little man. It was because of him that I had come to Sucre. His character had to reveal something about the country named for him. In addition to providing warmth, I expected Sucre to shed some light.

Gabriel pointed out Bolívar's portrait in the Casa de la Libertad—called such because it was here that Bolivia declared its independence. The leader looked oddly regal for a supposed republican: Bolívar Rex. The head was Roman—shaped like an acorn—and the ears surprisingly large. He stood brooding while behind him thunderheads massed.

Hair swept forward, he bore Napoleon a passing resemblance. Compare these two descriptions. First, Bolívar as seen by one of his generals: "He was five feet six inches tall, narrow-chested and slim, especially in the legs. His skin was dark and rather rough, his hands and feet so small that a lady might have envied them." And now Napoleon as biographer John Abbott described him: "His slight and slender figure [was] so feminine and graceful in its proportions; his hand so small, and white, and soft that any lady might covet it." The two men were equally vain. Bolívar had once refused to kiss the hand of Pius VII. And in 1822 he toasted Argentina's José de San Martín with the words, "To the two greatest men in the Americas: General San Martín and myself." One doesn't have to ask whom Bolívar considered the greater.

Both Bolívar and Napoleon were poorly educated. Simón Rodriguez, Bolívar's tutor and an admirer of Rousseau, taught him nothing—to preserve him in a state of nature. (Rodriguez established a school in Sucre shortly after independence. But his pedagogical methods met with little favor, and he left town somewhat hurriedly.)

Despite their similarities, Bolívar would have resented the comparison with Napoleon. Napoleon's continentalism had disenchanted him. His revolution would be different, Bolívar said. Though in the event this was not to prove the case.

When his idealism proved no match for South American realities, Bolívar showed himself Napoleon's equal in another respect: he could be no less imperious. Insisting that, unlike his rivals, he alone respected liberty of conscience, this effeminate little man—in England he was taken for a pederast—demanded unswerving loyalty. A poor example for Bolivia's new political elite, he was ruthless toward those who opposed his vision of a continental confederation. He made many enemies. So many, finally, they proved his undoing.

In the end his failure didn't surprise him. South America was full of crooks, he said. Dying of tuberculosis, he described himself as one of history's great idiots. Then, as his sickness entered its final stages, he pronounced South America a lost cause. Those who served the revolution had plowed the seas, he said. And died. He was forty-seven.

Bolívar's last words are so splendidly rhetorical that one suspects his ever having spoken them. (Napoleon's final utterance—"Josephine!"—is much more credible.) More likely they were coined later. An old tradition this, though not one on which we can always count. As recorded for posterity,

Pancho Villa's last words were "Please tell them I said something."

Gabriel captained a soccer team, and I was invited to watch one of their games. It was one of those five-on-a-side things: ten adults hurling themselves around a concrete basketball court with no concern for their safety and just an occasional glance at the gallery.

Were we looking?

Yes, we were.

They could proceed.

They played with absolute ruthlessness. They kicked and punched one another, shouldered and shoved, thumped and butted, elbowed and tripped. All to impress thirty spectators.

Were we looking still?

Yes, indeed. Much as one wanted to, it was impossible to look away.

Fired by our attention, they became more abandoned yet, performing new cruelties and even greater acts of recklessness. Soon all ten were hobbling around the court, four of them bleeding from the nose and two nursing their testicles. It was an altogether unwarranted show of ferocity. Nothing depended on the outcome of this game. It was what Gabriel had called "a friendly."

"Ten little Bolívars," said María, whom Gabriel had allowed to come along. It was her payment for giving him the loan he had been seeking. "They think they're being manly." She watched the game hardly at all, preferring to read a book.

Each side got along fairly well when the score was in its favor. But when it fell behind, the players fell to bickering, each blaming someone else for the reversal.

Gabriel, playing goalkeeper, let in one ball after another. But was the fault ever his? Never!

What was the fullback doing? he wanted to know. Where was the defense? Why wasn't someone stopping those balls before they reached him? He even blamed the goalposts—actually, heaped jackets—for his poor performance. The piles of jackets at his end of the court, he insisted, were farther apart than those at the other end. Nothing could convince him otherwise. Not even the tape measure the referee had with him. Having taken a position, he could not now abandon it, whatever the evidence. Losing face could not be countenanced.

Retiring to his goal, he addressed himself to the spectators. "Why do I get the feeling," he asked, "that I'm playing this game all by myself?"

The answer—and it can't have eluded him—was that all ten players saw this match as a solo turn. Teammates didn't simply compete against the opposing side; they fought one another just as fiercely. If there was glory to be had, each was resolved to be the one who'd have it. It was anarchy.

Gabriel's team lost—seven goals to three—and his captaincy was removed. He brooded all the way home on the bus. "I'm telling you there was something the matter with those jackets," he said. "But would anyone listen to me? Oh, no!"

If a tendency to deflect blame is Bolivia's tragedy, the refusal to admit that others might be right is Bolivia's vice. The outright rejection of opposing opinions is almost a point of honor. One's opponents cannot, must not be understood if one is to avoid appearing weak. One's own will is paramount and can't ever be frustrated.

Gabriel became more and more morose. His teammates had let him down, he said; they had betrayed him. They were no longer his friends; as of now they ceased to exist. He was doing what Bolívar had done—pronouncing enemies those who challenged his authority. The thought of being betrayed seemed to cheer him. Responsibility had been shifted again. After all, in a world in which a man can rely on no one but himself, could he be blamed for achieving little?

"I'm fortune's plaything," he said. The remark stirred María to pity.

"Poor Gabriel," she said, taking his hand. He placed his head in her lap. She was sitting with her legs on the seat facing ours. I saw his expression change when his glance fell on her damaged foot.

"I'm all right," he said, shaking himself free of her and sitting up. He stared ahead of him, saying nothing, for the rest of the trip.

I wanted to leave Sucre, but the *dueña* prevented it. Checking out, I asked if I might have my passport back. She had insisted I give it to her for safekeeping. She personally, she claimed, knew dozens of foreigners who had lost their passports in Bolivia. "And when I say lost," she confided, "I mean, of course, they were stolen."

What became of these people? To the best of her knowledge, they were in Bolivia still, roaming the country's frontiers, trudging wearily from border post to border post, and being turned back at all of them. "Just think," she said. "Never again will they see their families."

She no longer had my passport, it turned out. My room being burgled had unnerved her, and she had taken all she had of value—my travel papers included—to her bank.

"It'll come to no harm there," she said. "That bank has the biggest safe in the country. They keep the Declaration of Independence in it."

"The Declaration of Independence is in the Casa de La Libertad. I saw it myself."

"That's a photocopy," she said.

"Surely not. They keep it under lock and key."

She winked. "A safety measure," she whispered.

She said she would be happy to retrieve my passport for me—but right now there didn't seem much point.

"Why not?"

She glanced at her watch. "The bank is closed."

"But today is Friday. It doesn't open again until Monday."

"Tuesday," she said happily. The rolled newspaper had struck again. "Monday is a holiday."

She squealed suddenly and pointed. "Look at your bag lying in the lobby with no one watching it. Why, anyone could walk in here, and you'd never see it again. Take it to your room right now.

"And don't forget," she called after me as I made my way up the stairs. "Lock your door."

7

GABRIEL decided to come to Cochabamba with me. "I'm so glad I thought of this," he said, looking hugely pleased. "Tarata's near there; Melgarejo's birthplace. I can gather material for the play I'm writing. Soak up the atmosphere. Isn't that the expression?"

Mariano Melgarejo is Bolivia's most reviled figure, but Gabriel admired him, even keeping a picture of the former president above his bed. He looked like Prince Albert: a meek little man with diffident eyes and a massive beard.

"He doesn't look like a villain," I said.

"Of course not." Gabriel snorted. "History has done him a disservice. That's something I mean to correct."

His play finishes with Melgarejo lapsing into a coma after one of his drinking orgies. "But this is not to be taken literally," Gabriel said. "Actually, his coma is brought on because he despairs of ever reconciling Bolivia's interests with those of foreign capital."

Gabriel's company was not entirely welcome. Like him, I was going to Tarata—by now I too was under Melgarejo's power—but I wanted to go alone. From Tarata I had planned to go to Vallegrande. If I went to Vallegrande first, I could avoid hurting Gabriel's feelings.

"Come by all means," I told him, "but I'll be staying in Cochabamba no more than a day or two. I'm going on to Vallegrande."

"You can't be serious," he said, losing some of his ebullience. "If you go there, you'll be arrested."

On October 10, 1967, the Bolivian army invited reporters to Vallegrande to view the body of Che Guevara. Although the army had reason to exult, the officers who posed with the corpse appeared ill at ease. They might have been doctors explaining the loss of a patient who, for all their efforts, had stubbornly died on them.

The guerrilla had been executed a full twenty-four hours earlier. Even so, no one had thought to shut his eyes. Lying on a makeshift bier—a litter placed across a trough used for washing clothes—he looked more dazed than dead. One had the impression of a man taking an intense interest in his own postmortem. Clad only in trousers, Che's body looked slack, almost gross. The torso bore several bullet wounds—one just above the heart—and there were teeth marks on the right hand. When his executioner opened fire—Che was shot at point-blank range—the revolutionary had crammed his fingers in his mouth. An officer suggested that he may have been trying to stifle a scream.

To prevent Vallegrande from becoming a socialist Graceland, the army disposed of the corpse under cover of darkness. By one account, it was buried in an unmarked grave. By another, the body was cremated and the ashes scattered. Later the government took the additional precaution of placing Vallegrande off-limits to foreigners.

But that had been two decades ago. In the years since the Che legend had lost much of its potency. Even in Bolivia, where for so long just to mention him was deemed disloyal,

Guevara is again being discussed; just recently one of the country's bigger magazines had serialized his diaries. All in all, Gabriel's warning seemed exaggerated.

"You don't *really* think I'll be arrested, do you?" I asked him.

But he wouldn't discuss the matter. "I don't want to hear anything more about this," he said, putting his hands over his ears. "The less I know, the better. If you don't mind going to jail, well and good. But please: don't involve me."

I began to have qualms. And in Cochabamba there was further cause for disquiet. "Out of the question," said a bus official when I asked if I might travel to Vallegrande the following day, a Wednesday. His office was decked in plastic ivy, suggesting a recent bacchanal. "Try us on Friday."

This seemed odd, because the week's manifest lay open on the counter in front of me. From what I could see, there were seats galore. His making me wait, I concluded, could only mean that the authorities would have to be told about me. When I returned on Friday I would no doubt be met by police.

It wasn't a prospect I relished, but I would take my chances. Vallegrande appealed to my sense of irony. Che's plan for a revolution that would sweep the continent, toppling every autocratic institution in its path, had been ill conceived. Yet it was visionary too, and that it had ended the way it did seemed needlessly cruel—a cruelty emblematized by that laundry trough. I had to see it.

I was now presented with a more immediate problem: what to do until Friday. To the person killing time, Cochabamba offers limited opportunities. The country's third largest city, it is set in an area of farmland known as Bolivia's garden. The city itself, however, is far from beautiful.

A community founded in 1542 has certainly had time to cultivate its appearance, yet shabby Cochabamba seems not to have bothered. Virtually all its architectural treasures have been destroyed. Even the famed Church of La Merced. One of the loveliest buildings in the country, the three-hundred-year-old church was named a national monument in 1967. Yet just two years later it was torn down by order of the city to make room for an office block.

Nor does Cochabamba seem to have an intellectual life. The public library was empty the few times I was there, and the university, in an effort to draw students, had to offer a course in motorcycle mechanics. A professor I talked to complained that his charges grew more incurious by the day. "If I let them," he said, "they'd read only comic books." The few I was introduced to wanted to talk only about my sneakers. Where had I bought them? How much had they cost? Were they very comfortable?

Yet as a commercial center, Cochabamba is known for its dynamism. Located in one of the most fertile valleys in the country, it has fed the Altiplano for two centuries and has recently emerged as a center for light industry. Its exertions have made it relatively rich. The preponderance of beauty salons, the passion for warm-up suits, and the cars in its glutted streets all attest to the presence here of money.

"I defy anyone to come to Cochabamba and *not* get rich," said a Lebanese who'd emigrated to Bolivia sixteen years ago. "In a place like this, you just can't fail."

But if many regard its preoccupation with wealth as proof of this city's modernity, that preoccupation may also explain Cochabamba's relative lack of character. With prosperity has come uniformity, and a familiar uniformity at that. I was left feeling that here there are no ambiguities to resolve, no mysteries to plumb. There is only this unequivocal mercantile ethos.

"When Americans come to Bolivia, where do they feel most at home?" asked the Lebanese. "Here. Right here." I understood why: Madonna filled the newspapers, Cosby the air-waves, and the young, in jeans and high-tops, might have been teleported from Boston or Los Angeles.

But if Cochabamba is wealthier than Bolivia's other major cities, its poor seem more abject. In the plaza a woman said I might "take advantage" of her, as she put it, if first I bought her a beer. And later that same morning I rounded a corner in the Indian quarter, and there before me—the scene had something postapocalyptic about it—were nine squatting figures, all of them defecating.

Fortunately, Gabriel had an aunt here. Her name was Graciela, and without her my stay in Cochabamba would have been dull indeed. An herbalist, Graciela was a small, round woman with a nose like an overripe fig. In general appearance she suggested nothing so much as a series of interlocking spheres.

"Any aches or pains?" she asked when Gabriel introduced us in her small shop. Her tone was one more of hope than of solicitude.

I shook my head.

"Nothing at all? Arthritis? Indigestion? Stress? Sinus problems?"

I shook my head again.

"No allergies, varicose veins, hemorrhoids, cataracts, sores?"

"I'm sorry, but I'm perfectly well."

"Then why are you limping?"

"It's nothing much. An ingrown toenail. I'll be fine in a day or two."

Actually, the toe had hurt like the dickens for more than a week, and yesterday's primitive surgery—I had tried to cut the nail out—hadn't helped at all. The toe was now badly swollen and might even be septic.

"Better let me see it," said Graciela.

The look of it quite delighted her. "Oh, it's very bad," she said happily. "Unless you're careful, you'll lose that foot. You need one of my concoctions."

She prepared a poultice of coca leaves, and it worked wonders. In less than an hour the swelling had subsided and the pain had eased considerably.

"Where did you learn to do that?" I asked.

"Everything I know I learned from the Kallawaya Indians."

Bolivia's Kallawayas are itinerant folk curers whose prescriptions are famed through much of the continent. Their knowledge of herbs is said to be vast, yet some of their remedies lean toward the quaint. Their cure for headache, for example, is a dragonfly placed under the hat.

"It isn't everyone the Kallawaya take into their confidence," said Graciela. "They trusted me because I was nice to them. I learned all their secrets. We're almost friends."

"Almost?"

"Almost is as close as you'll get to a Kallawaya."

Like her mentors, Graciela relied heavily on coca leaves, prescribing them for everything from stomach ailments and rheumatism to gum infections and boils. Mixed with salt and egg whites, she said, coca leaves speed the recovery of broken bones. Coca leaves can do anything, she claimed—cure colds, improve the memory, even revive failing marriages.

"Revive them how?" I wanted to know.

"They're better than oysters," she said.

Graciela proved just as resourceful as a hostess.

"Have you heard of Klaus Barbie?" she asked the next morning.

"The Butcher of Lyons?"

"None other. I'll show you where he used to lunch."

Until his repatriation to France, Barbie, a former SS colonel, had lived in Bolivia for some thirty years. This had been no underground existence. Unlike those former Nazis who assumed new identities when they came to South America, Barbie made no secret of his background. Nor was he slow to offer his services: first to the army, whose counterinsurgency program he helped direct, then to cocaine czar Roberto Suárez, for whom he assembled a praetorian guard, and finally to Luis García Meza, whom he helped to power in 1980.

His lunch spot was surprisingly modest—a restaurant of twenty tables, each sporting a soiled gingham cloth and a water glass filled with paper napkins. (For economy each of the napkins had been cut in half.) The beaded curtain that normally separated kitchen and dining room was drawn back. A woman at the sink was peering at something she had taken from her nose. The proprietor stood by the front door, his arm on the cash register. He looked weary.

"He sat over there," said Graciela when we had ordered the specialty of the house—*pollo a la canasta* (chicken in a basket). The table to which she pointed was occupied by a woman who mistook our interest for an overture. "Shall I join you?" she called.

Did she realize she was sitting at Klaus Barbie's table, Graciela asked her when she sat down.

"Never heard of him," she said. "I've only just got here." From Minneapolis, she was a missionary, she explained.

"How nice," said Graciela. "You're a nun."

"Not exactly," said the woman. "I'm a Jehovah's Witness."

Without meaning to, Graciela hissed when the denomination was mentioned. Hearing herself, she slapped a hand to her mouth.

Was she making many converts? I asked the missionary.

"Not as many as I'd like," she said. "It's slow work. Why? Well, my Spanish isn't very good. And then there's that."

She pointed to a picture of the Madonna above the cash register.

"The locals call her the Virgin of Urqupina, and she's supposed to be the font of all riches. Which begs the question: Why, in that case, does Bolivia get poorer by the day?"

"Perhaps the riches are spiritual," I was about to say when Graciela interrupted me.

"When did you last go to the bathroom?" she asked, peering into the face of the newcomer. "Not for some time, right? I'd say you have worms. Lots of them. That's why you're so pale. I'm very good with worms. I have a shop around the corner. You should drop by sometime."

The evangelist looked at me, looked at Graciela, and then looked at me again.

"Is she serious?" she asked in English.

"I believe she is," I said.

"You see now what I'm up against," she said, getting to her feet and handing me a pamphlet. Something from Isaiah: "You will see no more the insolent people, the people of an obscure speech which you cannot comprehend, stammering a tongue which you cannot understand."

She began to give one to Graciela—and then thought better of it. "I really should be going," she said to me, still speaking in English. "I've lots to do. Maybe I'll see you around."

Time must have been weighing heavily on me because, when Gabriel suggested I go to Tarata with him the next day, I readily agreed.

Though now much diminished, Tarata must once have been quite lovely. Small—no more than a few hundred people live here—it is beautifully proportioned. Its streets switch back and forth, never quite deciding where they're headed, and its homes are modestly grand, their windows crammed with red geraniums, their eaves painted bright shades of blue and pink. Some houses have wrought-iron balconies, others friezes of vines and urns and scowling lions in low relief. And

although the balconies sag dangerously and the lions are missing chins, the dilapidation has something heroic about it.
Lesser structures, I couldn't help thinking, would have given
up the ghost a long time ago.

In the plaza Indian women at makeshift tables sold bread
and fruit. One of them was so old that when she struggled
to her feet she did so with all the difficulty of a newborn calf.
Nearby two teenage boys wrestled each other and overturned
a table of oranges. Neither bothered to apologize. They would
recently have discovered the privileges that attached to being
male in this society. Arrogance was their birthright.

The bottled-gas man arrived to such cheers you would have
thought he'd run a blockade to get here. The market women
crowded around his truck, chattering like cicadas. He was
quite the favorite. Yet much as they liked him, they must
have considered him something of a rogue. The cylinders he
offered them were all rejected.

"Give me that one," said a woman, pointing. "And the one
behind it."

When the cylinders were lowered to her, she tested them
for weight. Neither was to her satisfaction.

"Let me try the one in front of you," she said. "And the
one on your right as well."

Our own arrival caused an even greater stir. We virtually
brought Tarata to a standstill. Commerce was abandoned, it
was my impression, and the young released from school. People left their lunch tables to watch us pass. Standing in
doorways, they called to those still within to hurry if they
were not to miss us. Like two champion golfers, we were
followed everywhere by a small gallery which, try as we might,
we could not elude. It slowed when we slowed, quickened
its pace when we quickened *our* pace; and when we stopped
for tea, it sat patiently and waited until we'd finished.

The gallery included an extraordinary number of dogs. I

marveled that Tarata had survived their micturition. A timid-looking lot, they seemed a far cry from the canines used by the conquistadors to subjugate the Bolivian uplands. Since horses were of limited utility in this terrain, dogs—trained to eat their victims alive—became an important weapon in the arsenal of conquest. Such was their reputation for ferocity that Indians committed suicide—jumping to their deaths or hanging themselves—to escape them.

The Spaniards placed great value on these animals, but as their numbers grew they became something of a nuisance. In Lima dogs so proliferated that Thursdays were designated "dog-killing days." And once a year in Potosí, citizens were required to produce ten dead dogs apiece. Those who failed to do so were fined.

Several dogs had collected outside the former Palacio Consistorial. Now a cinema, it was showing something called *The Big Chief*—not the paean to Melgarejo we first thought it but one of those karate efforts in which Bruce Lee flails his arms and grunts a lot. As far as we could see, Melgarejo was not memorialized at all. And Gabriel was livid.

"I can't believe this," he said. "One of the most important figures in Bolivian history, and his hometown can't be bothered to raise a statue to him. Not so much as a bust."

"Perhaps there's a plaque somewhere," I said, more to mollify him than anything.

"You want to see a plaque?" said a member of the gallery. "There's one in the plaza."

But instead of Melgarejo, this plaque commemorated the visit here two years ago of a delegation from China—a country that had provided Tarata with many of its streetlights.

The absence of a memorial doesn't mean that Melgarejo has been forgotten. Everyone we met had a story about him. One man told of the time in 1870 when France declared war on Prussia and Melgarejo, ever the Francophile, vowed to render the French what assistance he could. Doubtless drunk, he rounded up his troops and set off across the Altiplano in the direction of Europe. What he would have done when he got there we shall never know because, fortunately for the Prussians, the expedition had not gone far when it began to rain, and Melgarejo, jealous of his comfort, ordered his soldiers back to their barracks.

Another told of Melgarejo returning to La Paz after touring the provinces to discover that a former president, Manuel Isidoro Belzú, had deposed him. Anticipating trouble, Belzú had filled Plaza Murillo with thousands of his followers. But Melgarejo was not cowed so easily. Drawing his pistol, he strode into the presidential palace and shot the interloper dead.

The gun still smoking in his hand, Melgarejo then addressed the mob. "Belzú is no more," he said. "Who rules Bolivia now?" The crowd pondered the question but a moment. "*Viva Melgarejo*," it called back. "*Viva la patria.*"

Melgarejo provoked scandal after scandal. He once tested a revolver by firing randomly into a crowded street, and women who took his fancy were seized and dragged to his bed. He gave parties at which his male guests were either made to dance with one another or required to watch with equanimity while his naked mistress vamped on a tabletop. Those who lost their composure—and these performances were designed for no other purpose—were brutally flogged.

At one of these parties, it is said, the British ambassador accused the president of being a cad and ordered him to mend his ways. Normally this would have earned the man a whipping. But given the ambassador's rank, Melgarejo decided to be lenient. Instead of being beaten, the offending diplomat was stripped, strapped to a donkey, and run out of town to the jeers of the rabble.

Queen Victoria was livid. Britain had been disgraced, she

said, and she ordered her ships to shell La Paz. Being told that the city was far inland and beyond the range of even British firepower only increased her fury, and, taking a pen, she struck Bolivia from the map. Melgarejo and the country he presided over had been consigned to oblivion.

This story, still told in Bolivia and widely believed, is apocryphal. Britain and Bolivia did quarrel, but the dispute had to do with trade and involved not Melgarejo but President Belzú, the man he would later murder. Belzú's decision to restrict the import of British manufactures so angered London that in 1853 it ordered its envoy to quit Bolivia altogether. Relations between the two countries would not be resumed until 1910.

Illegitimate, Melgarejo was abandoned first by his father and then by his mother. At age three he was alone in the world. The experience made him deeply suspicious. Not even the shirt on his back could be trusted, he said once. And then, to make his point, he pinned that unreliable garment to a wall and riddled it with bullets.

He saw allegiance as something one bought. His army of two thousand men boasted seven generals and over four hundred officers. All owed their positions to his patronage. Those whose loyalty seemed to waver were promptly retired— though with generous pensions. Disgruntled former officers are notorious for causing trouble. Money, it was hoped, would keep them quiet.

Until he finally came to power in 1864, Melgarejo made sedition his life's work. Involved in coup after coup, he was variously jailed (he escaped), exiled (he was recalled), and sentenced to death (he was granted clemency). Yet for all his treachery, he was not ungallant. When, in 1870, his enemies captured his mistress, he agreed to surrender the presidency if she were given safe passage to Peru. Shortly afterward he followed her into exile. But the gesture was lost on her. She refused to see him, and when one evening he forced his way into her home, her brother emptied a revolver into the former president's head.

It is said of Bolivia that to understand it, you must first understand Melgarejo. Of the nineteenth-century caudillos, he was the most notorious, and even today Bolivians can't quite decide whether to be amused by him or appalled. For some, he was a mestizo Quixote, who sought only to right society's wrongs. For others, he was rapacious and sadistic, a barbarian.

Demonstrating that greed alone doesn't qualify one to run a country, Melgarejo mortgaged Bolivia to foreign bankers and made concessions that would eventually cost the nation its Pacific seaboard. At times his actions were so reckless that he seemed intent on destroying this country. What surprises is that after him it would exist at all. Either indifferent to its interests or incapable of defending them, Bolivia under his rule became progressively smaller. In 1866 Melgarejo surrendered territory to Chile. A year later he ceded to Brazil much of Mamoré and the Beni. It is largely because of him that Bolivia today is half the size it was at independence.

His politics were primitive at best. As contemptuous of theory as he was of the average citizen, he said once, "You don't need books to govern a country of dunces." He was less cavalier about the army, on whose support he depended to stay in power. Military spending soared, financed—once the national treasury had been exhausted—by a debased currency, booty, and extorted loans. His troops roamed the country, looting and pillaging as they went. Whole towns were sacked. Even Tarata wasn't safe. In 1865 news of Melgarejo's approach was sufficient to send the population fleeing for the hills.

Melgarejo was a product of his times. When Bolivia gained its independence, the country was little more than a grab bag of warring regions. Self-rule caught it unprepared. It lacked political institutions, a governing class, a working constitution. Only the military could preserve the peace, and so it happened that he who ran the army ran the country. Force became the final arbiter. But force bred force. Tyranny begat revolution, and revolution begat tyranny. Insubordination was now a tradition.

It is small wonder that Belzú would pronounce Bolivia incapable of being governed. It was Belzú's belief that only a monarch could unite the country, and in 1849 he sent José Mascarenas to Europe with orders to find a suitable candidate.

Mascarenas's choice was the conde de Aquila, brother of Fernando II, king of Naples, and brother-in-law of Dom Pedro II, emperor of Brazil. But nothing ever came of it. La Paz rioted when it heard of Belzú's plan, and the scheme was quickly dropped.

For all Melgarejo's shortcomings, many Bolivians are slow to condemn him. The ruthlessness with which he clung to power has invested him with a perverse glamour. In many ways he exemplified the Spanish imperial spirit. While the struggle for independence was waged in the name of liberty, the *criollos* sought not so much a general freedom as the opportunity to replace Spanish rule with a rule of their own. The nature of that rule remained the same. After independence—no less than before—it was the instinct of those in power to impose their will.

Of itself the ability to force submission doesn't confer legitimacy. Because it invites challenge, authority in such cases can rarely maintain itself for very long. Inevitably those who wield power only do so until a greater force emerges to displace them. This makes it necessary for each new regime to discredit the one that went before. What this has produced is a recurring spectacle in which, one after another, Bolivia's leaders are accused of having betrayed the country. (In many cases "betrayal" constitutes nothing more grievous than an inflexibility forced on them by equally inflexible opponents.)

The virulence of these attacks must be unique. There is the example of Andrés Santa Cruz, one of the country's most capable presidents. In 1836 congress eulogized him as "an immortal hero," "an angel of peace chosen by God to staunch Bolivia's tears." Yet just three years later this same congress denounced him as a tyrant, an abominable monster, a devil, an insect, a wretch.

Between 1880 and 1940 five former presidents were required to answer charges that they had abused their powers. One wonders if there isn't about this something of the practice of those ancients who killed their leaders before age or death could enfeeble them. Or it may only be that Bolivians care little for stability.

"Emergency is a normal state of affairs for us," said the man who told us of Melgarejo's mad dash to save France. "Ours is a history of crisis. We've learned to enjoy it. It makes us feel important."

I was able to buy a ticket for Vallegrande the next morning—but in circumstances that were not encouraging. The ticket clerk summoned a colleague when I presented myself, and this older one asked to see my passport.

"This is a passport?" he said when I gave it to him. I think he may not have seen one before.

"I'll tell you what I'm going to do," he said. "I'll keep this until this evening. Come and see me before the bus leaves. I'll give it to you then."

This was most unusual. I had been taking buses in Bolivia for two months at this point, and until now no one had asked to *see* my passport, much less tried to impound it. I was reluctant to hand it over. For one thing, I feared never seeing it again; for another, the police will sometimes approach foreigners in the street and ask to see their documents. Have none, and they're likely to lock you up.

"If I give it to you, I won't be able to change a traveler's check at the bank," I said, improvising. "I'm completely out of money."

"Very well," said the clerk, drawing a pencil from behind his ear. "I'll just make a note of the number." He recorded not merely the number but the place and date of issue, my date of birth, my height, and the color of my eyes.

I left feeling a little bit concerned. Perhaps the authorities were to be apprised of my intentions after all. Vallegrande began to recede. Still, there was nothing for it but to wait. And I did have my ticket. That was something. In the meantime I would pass the day as pleasantly as I could.

I took myself to the plaza. In Bolivian cities the plaza enjoys a special prestige. It might be a large, communal drawing room, a club open to all. It's always crowded. In the morning it's a refuge for the old; in the afternoon, a playground for schoolchildren. At night it becomes the haunt of lovers. For these last, home provides just shelter. They repair to the plaza to do their living.

All the major institutions of power are represented in the plaza. There is City Hall, police headquarters, the cathedral. There may be a bank or two. And a theater. And a bandstand. The post office is usually here. And sometimes the library. The plaza is at the heart of things; it is the center, and everything—everyone—is drawn to it eventually. Its attraction won't be resisted.

It was still early when I got there, and the plaza was filled with elderly men. In pairs, they wandered arm in arm or sat and spoke in whispers, each with a hand on the other's knee. Near me two of them discussed the death of a contemporary.

"He shouldn't have died," said one, a man in his eighties. "He was younger than I am."

I bought oranges, bananas, and a small loaf of bread—sufficient for a picnic lunch—and headed for La Coronilla, a monument to the women who defended Cochabamba during the fight for independence. It is a grudging tribute. While Cochabamba's male heroes are celebrated in the central plaza, female heroism is relegated to this hill on the city's outskirts. And while La Coronilla is not unimpressive, towering over it is another male figure—the Sacred Heart.

The only people here were Indians, dozens of them, and all carrying cheap cameras. Approaching the monument, they removed their hats. But honoring female courage was not their only purpose. They had come too to take pictures of Cochabamba's airport, of which this hill provides a striking view.

There was a great stir when a plane edged onto the runway. And although it was some time before the plane took to the air, the Indians watched in silence until it had. Even then they kept their watch, staring as it climbed skyward, still straining to see it when it had cleared the surrounding hills and vanished from their view.

At La Coronilla one can breathe the purest air in the world, according to the tourist office. But my lunch was spoiled because the shrine has become another of Cochabamba's unofficial public toilets. The smell was impossible to escape, and there was aging excrement everywhere I looked. It was just a little off-putting, and I was forced to change my plans. There was a circus in town. Instead of having a picnic, I'd pay it a visit.

Doing so was no easy matter. The circus was encamped somewhere near the river. "Just follow the Sixth of August," I was told. The Sixth of August is one of Cochabamba's major streets, but I confused it with another, called the Fifteenth of August and later, when I realized my error, with a third called August Twenty-seventh.

Bolivian streets are frequently named for major dates in the country's history. In addition to the three just cited, Cochabamba has thoroughfares called the Fourteenth of January, the Ninth of April, the Twenty-fifth of May, and the Sixteenth of July. And Cochabamba is not alone in this nomenclature. History has provided La Paz with names for at least four of its major arteries: the Sixteenth of July, the Sixth of August (Independence Day and a popular choice), the Twenty-sixth of August, and the Twentieth of October. And in Potosí, to cite one more example, the past is honored in the names the city gives its plazas: the Tenth of February, the Fifteenth of April, the Sixth of August (again), the Twenty-fourth of September, and the Eighteenth of November.

A further complication is that schools, hotels, restaurants, hospitals, and clinics are also sometimes named for dates. As with so much else in Bolivia, nomenclature simply obfuscates. How else to explain the decision to name three farming colonies—all founded at the same time and all within a short distance of one another—General Busch, Central Busch, and German Busch?

I found the circus after much searching, and it was well worth the trouble. The Circo Africa was a local affair, despite its international pretensions and its claims to include acts from Spain, Italy, Colombia, Mexico, and Chile. Nor was it terribly professional. Lupita of Mexico fell off the high wire— a drop of just 5 feet—when she tripped on her skipping rope; Señor Sánchez of Seville proved a churlish clown; the elephant was short a tusk; and the lions were so heavily sedated that it was all their trainer could do to keep them awake in the ring.

But for Ninotchka, it would all have been dreadful. An aerial artist, Ninotchka was Colombian, we were told, and I quite fell in love with her. She was no better than her colleagues, but while the others didn't mind not being good, Ninotchka, it was clear, minded very much. Desperate to excel, she put enormous effort into her performance. To no effect. The truth was she would never amount to much. Quite simply, she lacked talent. And yet she strove mightily. Ninotchka belonged with those stouthearted women commemorated on La Coronilla.

I could feel her longing. Had she only been capable of it, she would have moved the stars to tears. She would have taken wing and swooped above our heads. She would have soared and made us doubt our eyes. She would have mesmerized us, left us breathless. Clinging to her trapeze, she seemed suddenly such a small, lonely figure that I thought my heart would break.

Later Lupita, no worse for her tumble, walked through the audience selling pictures of herself. I rather hoped that Ninotchka might too. But she didn't.

Afterward I walked back to Calle Aroma. It was from here that the intercity buses left. It was almost seven—my bus would leave in an hour—and I stopped to have my shoes polished.

"How long are you staying in Cochabamba?" asked the shoeshine man. I knew him slightly. He had polished my shoes several times before.

"I leave this evening," I said, well aware that events might prove me wrong. I still didn't know what fate waited for me on the bus. Arrest? Incarceration?

The man grabbed my ankle. "You can't leave now," he said. "Look. I bought this just for you."

He held out a can of cordovan shoe polish. It must have cost him a day's wages, and for a moment I had a vision of myself forced to stay in Cochabamba until the polish ran out. And then perhaps he would buy another can, and I would be compelled to stay even longer. I had no choice but to buy it from him.

It was now eight o'clock, and thirty drivers had taken their places at the wheels of thirty buses. The street was jam-packed. Great drama attends these departures. These aging buses might be so many ocean liners, and instead of La Paz, or Santa Cruz, or Vallegrande, they might be headed for the Seychelles, or Bermuda, or Capri.

There was a sense of growing panic. Everyone talked at once, calling instructions above the hubbub, shouting words of warning, offering advice. People made their farewells as if they were parting forever. They wept uncontrollably or clung to one another, refusing to be separated. You would have thought we were going to certain death.

I boarded my bus expecting to be ordered off at any moment. All the seats were now filled, and two men—part of the overflow—sat on the floor and began to giggle. Luggage was still being handed up to a man on the roof: a sack of potatoes, a kitchen table, four trussed chickens, a fighting cock.

Hawkers filled the aisle. "Oranges and bananas," they called. "Bananas and oranges." Over and over. None of the passengers made a move, but the hawkers waited. They knew they had only to bide their time. Three minutes went by before a man asked, "How much are the oranges?" And then everybody wanted some.

"Two oranges for me."

"Four oranges over here."

"Give me four as well."

"I'll take six."

People quarreled over who should be sitting where; the driver announced a delay because his brakes didn't work; and it was discovered that much of the luggage on the roof belonged on another bus. And then, almost without anyone noticing, the driver was at the wheel again, the hawkers were told to leave, and the door was shut. We were on our way. And just an hour late too.

There was a problem, though. One of the hawkers had ignored the order to disembark, and the bus had left, taking her with it. She pleaded with the driver to let her off, but he pretended not to hear. Instead of slowing down, he accelerated. The men crowded around his seat greatly enjoyed this, slapping their thighs in merriment. The woman became increasingly frantic, no doubt imagining herself ending up in Vallegrande. As she might have, had the female passengers not intervened on her behalf.

The journey was miserable. All the windows had been shut tight—the one nearest me couldn't be opened because it didn't have a handle—and it became hellishly hot. And then, to make matters worse, the bus filled with gasoline fumes. The thought of having to endure this for twelve hours made me giddy with panic. I began to sweat.

The woman beside me watched me warily. I could hardly blame her. My comb had slipped out of my pocket when I came on board, and I'd had to lean past her to pick it up. But instead of saying *"Disculpeme; he dejado caer mi peine"*— Excuse me, I've dropped my comb—I said, *"Disculpeme; he dejado caer mi pene"*—Excuse me, I've dropped my penis. After a mistake like that, it seemed better to ignore her. In sleep, though, she became a little more animated. Drawn by my body heat, she snuggled against my shoulder and uttered those little yelping noises that, in some women, signal the approach of pleasure.

Eventually the suffocating heat produced a kind of stupor, and I managed to fall asleep myself. An hour later I was shaken awake. The bus had stopped, and a soldier was standing over me. My heart sank. It looked as if the jig was up.

But he wanted only to see my luggage. He and a colleague were searching bags in case any of us harbored cocaine.

At midnight we stopped in a small village for supper. Like many places its size, it owed its tenuous existence to the exigencies of bus travel. If buses hadn't stopped here occasionally, it might never have been summoned into being. Buses mean not only people stretching their legs and voiding their bladders but people eager for tea and sandwiches, hot meals and beer. Meager commerce, but because of it this hamlet now boasts a dozen houses and a church. And while it still looks rather miserable, the hamlet down the road—which buses bypass—looks more miserable still.

The rest of the journey was made additionally unpleasant because a truck had fallen across the road. It was much too dangerous to make a way around it in the dark. All we could do was wait for morning. But I'd stopped thinking of my own discomfort. A baby on board had a frightful cough. And it was breathing badly. Perhaps it had pneumonia. It might even have been dying. Yet it didn't once cry. A beautiful child. I thought of those ghastly white boxes I had seen in the La Paz cemetery and wished to God there was something I could do to help.

We reached Vallegrande four hours late. Not that I cared. I was happy to have got here at all. But I remained apprehensive. I still didn't know if my presence was welcome. My first impression was that it wasn't. At the sight of me, a child fled, a dog barked, a man glared, an old woman slammed her door shut, and a cyclist collided with a tree. And then I turned a corner and there, rushing in my direction, was a policeman.

I rehearsed the cover story I had prepared on the bus. I would say that I'd come to visit the Inca ruins at nearby Samaipata—a town, incidentally, that Che held briefly during his short campaign. But the policeman strode past without so much as glancing at me. I felt suddenly cross. I had begun to relish being a security threat. I consoled myself that he was very young. He couldn't have been in uniform long. Very likely he didn't know that foreigners were barred from here. This seemed to be confirmed a little later, when the policeman hurried toward me once again. With him this time was a more senior colleague. But I was not to be arrested even now. They had bigger fish to fry. They were off to the market for an early lunch.

Vallegrande now seemed more benign. The woman sweeping the street with a palm frond smiled when I wished her good morning, and when I entered the church the ten shawled women attending mass barely looked up.

The priest was very old. When he genuflected, an altar boy had to pull him to his feet. And when, during the consecration, he raised high the host, an acolyte stood on either side of him in case he lost his balance. Old as he was, he hadn't forgotten Che. In his sermon he inveighed against "foreign ideologies." Each one of us is unique, he told his listeners, and this was why the pope opposes the class struggle while supporting the struggle for justice. "The first pits man against man," he said, "while the second mobilizes all that's good in each of us." One of the congregants rolled her eyes.

The buildings in the plaza had been painted vivid shades of pink and green, but despite this—and the cow tethered to a tree outside the church—there seemed little to distinguish Vallegrande. Had the army not exhibited Che's body here, this small, rutted town would be unknown outside its immediate vicinity.

It was on October 8, 1967, that the army, acting on a tip from local peasants, surrounded Che and his guerrillas in a ravine outside Higuera, a town of three hundred people.

"Don't shoot," he told his captors. "I'm worth more to you alive."

Those who saw him said he looked sick and weak. Dogged

by hunger all year, he and his followers had had to forage for food. Traps were set, though never with much success. One day they caught a cat. If they were lucky, they managed to shoot something. In his diary Che wrote of once bagging four hawks. "They were not," he wrote, "as bad as might be imagined." The guerrillas were to become so desperate for food that eventually they would butcher Chico—the mule on which Che rode when his asthma made it impossible for him to walk.

For some time his asthma had been chronic. Months earlier the army had found his headquarters and seized his medicines. For relief now he would hang from a tree or have his colleagues pound his chest. He might, more simply, have mixed coca leaves with sugar—a standard remedy for asthma in Bolivia. That he didn't know this says something about the haste with which he launched his guerrilla war.

As Che was led into Higuera after his capture, a group of Indian women demanded his execution. "Kill him," they shouted. "Kill him now." Yet according to witnesses, Che appeared calm. He may still have thought that his celebrity would save him. It was not until the next day that he spoke of dying. "I want to die on a full stomach," he said, and asked for something to eat. By then the order had come from La Paz to kill him.

The man who volunteered to shoot Che was Warrant Officer Mario Teran. Shortly after lunch Teran entered the schoolhouse in which the guerrilla was being held. He was carrying an M-2 carbine. Teran must have suffered a momentary loss of nerve, because he was seen to hurry out a moment later, collect himself, and then go in again. Shortly afterward shots were heard.

Che's body was flown to Vallegrande and displayed on that infamous laundry trough. Perhaps it too was disposed of secretly. Burned and its ashes scattered. Or interred in an unmarked grave. In any event, much as I looked, I couldn't find it.

It didn't matter. I no longer wished to see it. Thinking about it now, I saw that Che's plan to bring down a continent wasn't visionary at all. It was preposterous—as silly in its way as Melgarejo rushing to the aid of France. Che knew little about this country he sought to save. He misread its geography, its army, and its people. He misread too the impact of the revolution. He seems not to have considered that the Indians mightn't rally to him—even though, as landowners, they now had a stake in the status quo. Che failed to recruit a single Indian, and that fact, more than any other, made defeat inevitable.

He was equally contemptuous of Bolivia's left wing. The country's radicals were intensely nationalistic, and much as they desired a communist takeover, it had to be one in which they played a significant part. But Che refused to share authority. Any leadership other than his own was unacceptable. It seems extraordinary, but when he died no one was more relieved than Bolivia's communists.

Che has been called a warrior-apostle, an adventurer-prophet, a new Bolívar, a modern Christ. But most often his admirers have sought to depict him as a latter-day Quixote. Which was how he saw himself. When he left Cuba in 1965, he wrote to his parents, "I can feel Rocinante's ribs beneath my heels again."

Melgarejo too saw himself as a Don Quixote. As did Bolívar, and Santa Cruz, and Belzú, and most of Bolivia's other leaders—the current president among them. The knight of the sad countenance has had an extraordinary impact on the sensibility of this country. Would it have fared better had Cervantes not provided it with so compelling a model? The question is ironic because Cervantes once asked the Spanish Crown for a job in La Paz. Had he been given it, he would have had little time to write, and *Don Quixote* might not now exist.

The bus to Santa Cruz left Vallegrande on the dot, but we arrived considerably behind schedule. A section of the road was being resurfaced, and when the work crew failed to clear a way for him, our driver—independent even by Bolivian standards—became angry and blew his horn. The foreman didn't like this at all.

We were allowed to pass finally, and soon afterward the foreman overtook us in a pickup truck. He was in quite a hurry, but I thought little of it until we rounded a corner some time later, and there he stood—in the middle of the road. Behind him were two bulldozers and several tons of gravel. Our way was completely barred. The bulldozers now began an unusual game of tennis, pushing the gravel back and forth between them while the Indians on the bus, entirely innocent of any offense, sat quietly in their brown, lacquered seats and baked in the afternoon heat.

Our driver tried to tough it out. Looking as if he welcomed this delay, he drummed his fingers on the globular head of his stick shift—a globe, I'd noticed earlier, that glowed red when he changed gears. Peer into this crimson orb and one saw a Star of David.

But an hour later the bulldozers were still playing tennis, and our driver had had enough: He blew his horn again. Predictably, this only made the foreman angrier. A truck was brought up to reinforce the barricade, lest, I suppose, we were tempted to storm it. And then, in case that weren't enough, a tractor arrived as well.

A second hour went by. In the bus the passengers, none of whom had even mentioned this delay, stared out at the finger-splayed cacti bordering the road. A third hour passed. And then there chanced along a car also going to Santa Cruz.

Luckily for us the driver was a *criollo*, and the foreman, reluctant to inconvenience a "white," ordered the barricade removed.

We reached Santa Cruz nearly five hours late. Not one of the passengers expressed the mildest complaint.

8

I HAD BEEN in Santa Cruz five minutes when someone offered to sell me coke. Waiting for my bag to be unloaded, I was reading a guidebook when a man approached. "Need any help?" he asked.

"I'm looking for a cheap hotel."

He suggested I try *el centro*, the center—the area around the main plaza.

"How do I get there?" I asked him.

"Easy. Santa Cruz is built like this." Using a finger, he drew a circle on the palm of his hand. "The center is in the middle."

He laced his fingers and made his knuckles snap. "By the way," he said, "want to buy a gram?"

"No, thank you."

"A kilo, then? A gram, a kilo; I can get you any quantity you want."

I was made a similar offer in the taxi into town. Addressing his rearview mirror, the driver wanted to know (1) my views on Israel; (2) whether socialism was anything more than an ideal; (3) did the world have a future; and (4) would I care to buy some *cristal puro*? "Good stuff," he added.

Others dispensed with preliminaries altogether. "Snort?" asked people, stopping me in the street. And in case I wondered what *snort* meant, they would wriggle their noses and sniff like bloodhounds. Sometimes this pantomime was more graphic still, with a fist raised to the nostrils to suggest coke taken from the back of the hand.

One drug dealer gave me his business card. "Call me anytime," he said. "If I'm not home, leave a message with my daughter." And in the Gandhi—where I had gone for dinner—I was forced to leave when two dealers came to blows because they couldn't agree on who had seen me first.

The barber, the shoeshine boy, the man from whom I bought a newspaper—all tried to sell me coke. "A word of advice," said the newspaper vendor. "Buy a kilo; anything less simply isn't worth the trouble." I even had dealers call at my hotel. Three times that first day a maid came to my room with the news that "a gentleman" waited downstairs to see me.

Because Santa Cruz is the capital of the coke industry, no one would believe that I had come here for any other reason than to launch a career in drugs.

There was nothing clandestine about any of these approaches. There are those who sell coke, and there are those whose job it is to stop them. Yet the two groups are not the archenemies one might suppose. The law is enforced with no great vigor because the enforcers believe that, insofar as it pertains to drug trafficking, the law is an ass.

"We see nothing reprehensible in what we're doing," said Tom, a dealer I met in the plaza. "We're simply operating by the rules of a free market. The world wants cocaine, and we're in a position to supply it. Everyone prospers—not least the police."

A sloth stirred in the branches of the tree behind him.

"Besides, I doubt if there's anyone in this town who doesn't derive some of his income from coke. What are the police to do? Lock *all* of us up?"

A jeep drew to a halt in front of us, and the money changers across the street began to caw like crows.

"Watch this," Tom said, winking. "A little money laundering." I can't say how much was being traded, but each of these changers rarely carries less than five hundred dollars in pesos. On this occasion the man in the jeep cleaned out all twenty of them. "The tip of the iceberg," said Tom. "This industry brings in a billion dollars every year. Most of it ends up in Switzerland."

An Englishman, Tom spent part of the year in Santa Cruz selling coke, the rest in London, where he lived next door to Charlie Watts. When he got the chance, he said, he wrote poetry. He also maintained a correspondence with William Burroughs. His hobby was collecting first editions.

"Isn't that rather expensive?"

"Oh, I make a bit of money," he said. "Though the ones who get really rich are the people I sell to. We have clients in forty-seven cities round the world. I'll bet you know some of them."

He seemed dangerously loose lipped.

"Aren't you concerned that I might be a drug agent?"

"You mean DEA? God, no. All those people think about is nabbing Roberto Suárez. They couldn't care less about the rest of us. But I don't have to worry, in any event. I have connections."

The people for whom he worked—he referred to them as his family—had paid protection money. And just to be safe, Tom had befriended the head of the local Interpol station. "I've got him out of a scrap or two. I don't expect any trouble from that quarter."

He claimed to have access to figures at the pinnacle of the drug hierarchy. He could even introduce me to Suárez, if I wished, he said. But although I was to remind him of this offer several times, nothing ever came of it. Tom, I would find out, was at best a peripheral figure, and Roberto Suárez was far beyond his reach.

He was beyond the reach of most. Bolivia's most wanted man, Suárez has isolated himself in a remote part of the Beni—an area in which the government has little authority—and there fashioned his own polity. This state within a state has its own schools, its own clinics, its own army trained in Libya, and its own air force—a fleet of modern fighter-bombers each carrying air-to-air missiles.

Many—and marvelous—are the stories told about this man, whose great-grandfather was Bolivia's first ambassador to Britain. He is said to sleep holding a gold-plated revolver; on his birthday he disburses money from his private plane; and his constant companion is a leopard on whom he lavishes the most expensive gifts. By one account, this animal even has its own car—although no one could tell me if it had ever learned to drive. Rumor has it too that Suárez is highly sensitive and won't be described as a drug lord. He prefers the term *agroindustrial entrepreneur*.

There are still those who regard him as a benefactor. He is given credit for building roads and providing the poor with radios. On top of which, he is anti-American—no small thing in Bolivia. In 1982, when his son was arrested in Switzerland and extradited to Miami to face drug-smuggling charges, Suárez offered himself in exchange if the U.S. government would agree to pay Bolivia's foreign debt. Washington ignored the offer, proving—said Suárez—that its talk of stamping out the drug trade was all a sham.

The incident made him popular for a time. But Bolivia quickly tires of its heroes, and many now resent him. Suárez, who supplies one-third of all the cocaine entering the United States and makes an estimated $500 million a year, has been too successful for too long. Heroes are supposed to overreach themselves, to fail spectacularly. By contrast, Suárez only grows richer and more powerful.

Yet his success has been bought at some cost. There is a little of Howard Hughes about him. A near recluse, he has become frail and emaciated and is rumored to be a drug addict. He has also become increasingly distrustful, firing associates whose loyalty he questions, and obsessed with eluding those who seek his capture. He divides his time among his many ranches, arriving unannounced, departing again a day later with no word as to where he might be going. The pathos of flight. (Suárez's luck ran out in July 1988, when government troops surrounded one of his homes and took him captive. He is now being held in La Paz.)

While cocaine is this city's major source of wealth, there are others too. Santa Cruz is the capital of a region which, as well as being rich in oil, has recently become a major producer of cotton, sugar, rice, and coffee. With a population of 600,000, it is now Bolivia's second largest city and by far its most prosperous—a dramatic turnaround for a place that just fifty years ago was dismissed as moribund.

All this new wealth has given Santa Cruz the voice in national affairs it had long sought. Yet many here have still to be convinced that the central government takes their aspirations seriously, and they wonder if the region wouldn't be better served if it broke with Bolivia altogether.

"You've been to La Paz," said Adolfo, a restaurateur and ardent separatist. "So you know how little we have in common with those people. The Altiplano is one country, and we are another. We occupy different worlds. Our history is different, our culture, our traditions. Even our Indians are different. How? They don't mind working. There's no greater difference than that!"

Adolfo was a small man with one shoulder much higher

than the other. He looked as if he were permanently warding off attackers.

"Have you finished lunch?" he asked. "Good. I want to show you something."

He led me into a small office, where he opened a drawer and pulled out a flag—a gold crown and cross on a green-and-white background. "This is the flag of the sovereign nation of Santa Cruz. I want you to remember it. You'll be seeing it again."

An independent Santa Cruz, he said, would be the richest country in South America.

"This would be no Third World state, I assure you. Without La Paz to siphon off our wealth, we'd have the highest standard of living on the continent. Does Bolivia need us? Of course it does! Do we need Bolivia? Not in the least! Do we owe Bolivia any loyalty? None at all! For four hundred years La Paz ignored us. And if oil hadn't been found here thirty years ago, it would be doing so still."

The central government claims that sentiments like these are being fostered by Brazil, which it suspects of wanting to absorb the region. Why? Oil for one thing. Brazil has little to speak of. Markets for another. As Brazil industrializes, it must find more outlets for its manufactures.

Brazil's interest in Santa Cruz became apparent in 1971, when it helped overthrow the government of President Juan José Torres. During his ten months in power, Torres had expelled the Peace Corps, stepped up contacts with Moscow, annulled mining contracts with the United States, and founded a "popular assembly," which was to function as a kind of soviet. None of this endeared him to the military regime in Brasília. Fearing another Cuba, Brazil began channeling money to General Hugo Banzer Suárez. Banzer Suárez tried to depose Torres in January 1971—and failed. He tried again seven months later, and this time succeeded. Immediately afterward Brazil established what it called a "pole of development" in Santa Cruz. Much Brazilian money was invested in the area, and the number of Brazilian nationals grew. Many of them, it is said, are illegal immigrants.

La Paz views this trend with mounting concern. Some government officials even warn of "another Acre"—Acre being the territory annexed by Brazil in 1903, after its nationals poured into the area at the height of the rubber boom.

To offset Brazil's influence, La Paz has adopted the strategy of opening up the region to settlers from the Altiplano. But *cruceños*, now more distrustful of the government than ever, see another motive. "It's not Brazil they're trying to offset," said the impassioned Adolfo. "It's us. By filling the place with Aymara, they hope to outnumber us. Well, it won't work. This movement gets stronger all the time. If we ever decide to, we can make this place ungovernable."

Santa Cruz was founded in 1561 by a Spanish adventurer looking for the mythic riches of El Dorado. He died a broken man, but it must console his shade that the city he started would itself become identified with fabulous wealth, a place reminiscent of Potosí in its heyday. Coke millionaires abound here and, under their influence, Santa Cruz has become ever more incongruous.

In a city once known for colonial color, what strikes one now are its many odd conjunctions: modest stucco houses under the lee of modern office blocks; coca leaves and expensive male toiletries side by side in the market; the makeshift homes of the poor contrasting with the pseudobaronial manses of the well-to-do; the conspicuous consumption of the arrivistes and the equally conspicuous austerity of the Mennonites.

The Mennonites are particularly startling. The women are scrupulous in their avoidance of glamour. They wear plain black stockings and plain black shoes and dresses that, if you ask, they will tell you they made themselves. By hand in some cases. The more traditional of them even eschew sewing machines. Their husbands are a little more progressive. Although many of them shun the telephone and have still to see a film, they haven't hesitated to mechanize their farms. They had no choice, one man told me. "Manual labor is impossible to get," he said. "The coke industry has pushed wages so high, we can no longer compete."

A man with a bright red face, he wore a straw hat and blue coveralls and looked for all the world like the farmers one sees in parts of Texas. He was in town to negotiate a bank loan, he said. "I don't like Santa Cruz. If I didn't need a new tractor, I wouldn't be here at all. I stay away as much as I can. We all do."

For many *cruceños*, Mennonite exclusivity is a source of rancor. Mennonites are charged with having too much power—another state within a state—and too much money. Others accuse them of refusing to share their expertise, of enriching themselves while contributing little to the local economy. What's more, they're said to disdain Bolivia. According to Adolfo, many Mennonites continue to speak low German and often insist that their Indian workers do so too.

"We're supposed to be arrogant," said the red-faced man whose name I never learned, "but all we want to do is preserve our traditions. We have to keep our distance."

This man, along with two thousand of his coreligionists, moved to Santa Cruz from Mexico twenty years ago. "We had a thriving community in Mexico. But our numbers grew, and land got scarce. That's why we came here. To found new colonies. The government promised to stay out of our way."

And had it?

"They don't bother us."

Born in Manitoba in 1930, he was twelve when he and his parents moved to Mexico—forced out of Canada by the threat of government interference. "There was a war on," he said, "and there was talk of making us enlist. Well, Mennonites don't hold with killing. We're pacifists. We got out while we could."

Until now the Mennonites have prospered in Santa Cruz. But he saw that changing. "The whole area is overproducing," he said. "Go into the countryside and you'll see crops rotting in the fields. They're not worth harvesting because the market is saturated."

Why not export?

"Transportation. By the time you've paid shipping costs, you have a product that's so expensive no one wants to buy it."

Was there a chance, then, that the Mennonites might leave Bolivia as they had once left Mexico, and before that Canada?

"Eventually, perhaps, but no time soon. Life here is hard, but it has its compensations. I belong to a close-knit community, and my children are being raised in the proper way."

What way was that?

"The way laid down in the Bible."

Tom turned up at my hotel the next evening looking jubilant. It was the first time I'd seen him in more than a week.

"I've been away on business," he said, winking. "Very profitable business. I'm in a mood to celebrate." He slapped his hands. "What do you say we do some lines?"

"Why not?" I said. One is only human.

"I didn't expect to find you here," he said, rolling a twenty-dollar bill. "I was sure you'd have left by now."

"Why?"

"There isn't much to do in Santa Cruz. You must be bored to death. I know what I'll do: I'll show you our night spots. I'd arranged to meet a friend. We can bring him along."

We found José having dinner in a restaurant across the street.

"Meet the best pilot in Bolivia," Tom said, introducing him.

"The best *unemployed* pilot in Bolivia," José corrected him. "If I don't get a job soon, I'll have to move to Miami."

"Why there?" I asked.

"Pilots are never stuck for work in Miami," he said. "Lots of drug runs."

For now though José was preparing what he called "a big one"—in a month's time he planned to smuggle 20 kilos of coke into France. I was startled that he would tell this to me, a complete stranger. But I apparently had his confidence.

"The risks are very great," I said uneasily. Did his sharing this information make me an accomplice?

"Not for me," he said. "I have a friend in French customs."

"Besides," said Tom, "if there were no risks, what would be the point in doing it?"

José expected to make several million dollars on the deal— a decent return for a day's work. What would he do with it?

"First, I'll go to India and spent a year or two there. And after that, I'll go to Greece."

But couldn't he go to both these places without risking his liberty?

"This way is more fun," he said.

Tom left to talk to four teenage boys at the next table. They had ordered a substantial dinner, and I was a little concerned for them. This restaurant, though unexceptional, was not cheap. But the bill presented no problem. They were rolling in money.

"You know them?" I asked Tom when he came back.

"Two of them work for a friend of mine," he said.

"Doing what?" I asked.

"They tread coca leaves. To release the cocaine, the leaves

have to be soaked in kerosene and then trod on for several hours. That's what they do. Their feet are their fortune."

"I think I've heard that most of them develop skin cancer," I said.

He shrugged. "They know what the dangers are. Besides, what do you think would happen if I went over there and said, 'Look, chaps, this work you do is far too risky; I'm going to have to lay you off'? I'd be lucky to escape with my life."

The three of us adjourned to the bathroom and did more lines.

"This is good stuff," said Tom. "If you'd like to buy some, I can get you a matchboxful for twenty dollars. Yes? Right, then. Wait for me at the table. I'll be back in thirty minutes."

An hour later he had still to reappear, and José was fuming.

"Do you trust that man?" he wanted to know.

"Why, yes," I said. "At least, I think I do. I rather took him at face value. Was that wrong?"

"He's a liar and a fantasist."

"Charlie Watts is not his neighbor? He doesn't collect first editions?"

"Don't make me laugh. Have nothing to do with him. I'd hate to see you land in trouble."

"You can't be serious."

"Stay away from him. Has he suggested that you courier for him?"

"Courier what?"

"Coke. What else has any value around here?"

"No, he hasn't."

"Well, he will, believe me. And when he does, if you have any sense, you'll tell him to fuck himself."

"But I thought you and he were friends," I said.

"You can't be friends with a junkie."

"Tom isn't a junkie!"

"Why do you think he stays in Santa Cruz?"

I had imagined coke addicts to look much as the nineteenth-century Swiss scientist von Tschudi described them: "They have bad breath, pale lips and gums, greenish and stumpy teeth, and an ugly black mark at the angles of the mouth." On top of which their gait is unsteady, their skin yellow, and each of their "sunken eyes encircled by a purple ring."

Tom turned up two hours later, by which time José had turned murderous. And it didn't help that the coke he brought fell far short of filling a matchbox.

"You rotten son of a bitch," said José. "This had better be good, because, if it isn't, I'll have you destroyed."

"Now that's a man I wouldn't want to cross," said Tom. José had taken the coke to the bathroom. "A nasty piece of work. If you take my advice, you'll steer clear of him."

He then proceeded to warn me against José in much the same terms José had used when warning me against him. He was dangerous and untrustworthy; it was impossible to believe anything he said; he was a coke addict—"and you know what they're like"—and, what was more, Tom had it on good authority that José was a police informer.

"Has he asked you to courier for him?"

"No, he hasn't."

"Give him time. He will."

A woman leaned over us.

"Buy me a drink," she said.

"Ignore her," said Tom. "She has the clap. In this town, pure women are as rare as honest men."

For all his talk of being rich, he hadn't a penny to his name. I ended up buying Tom's dinner. José's too. He had no money either. He asked to borrow twenty dollars.

"Until you get a job in Florida?"

"Until I pull the big one."

Later that evening José did suggest that I courier for him. Just as Tom had predicted. And shortly after that, Tom suggested that I courier for *him*. As José had said he would.

It was Tom who advised me to keep the coke I'd bought in my underpants.

"It's the one place a Bolivian policeman won't look," he said.

It struck me later that, were I being set up, his advice would make a search of my person relatively easy.

Perhaps I *shouldn't* trust him. Or José, for that matter. But if not them, who? No one? I felt suddenly paranoid. I convinced myself that I was followed back to the hotel, that the car parked across the street had been trailing me all day. I went upstairs and concealed my 3 grams of contraband in one of the public toilets. They could search me now, if they wished. I was clean. But I still felt threatened. I lay awake for hours, and when, at last, I did fall asleep, I dreamt that my door had been kicked in and a policeman was holding a gun to my head.

When I woke the next morning, my coke was no longer where I'd put it. But there was no time to dwell on that. More important things were afoot. With American assistance, the Bolivian army had begun a series of raids on cocaine laboratories in the Beni. Even though the action had been anticipated for weeks, Santa Cruz was stunned. Not only had a foreign power intervened in Bolivian affairs, there were the consequences for the city's economy to consider.

"We have been invaded," a grim-faced man said at breakfast.

The others at his table nodded. They looked ashen. Wild rumors began to circulate: The Americans planned to spray the area with Agent Orange; the laboratories were to be bombed; the jungle would be napalmed; the Beni would be made a wasteland. Not a tree or a bird would be left in that vast place.

Again and again I was asked to explain the American action. Since I was a foreigner, it was assumed I would support it.

"Why would they do this?" asked Adolfo. "Are we forcing cocaine on a captive public? Five million Americans use cocaine because they want to. If they didn't, there wouldn't be a cocaine industry. We didn't create this demand. All we're doing is meeting it."

He said President Reagan was being cynical. "If he's serious when he says drugs are a health hazard, why doesn't he ban cigarettes? If he's serious when he says the drug trade is threatening American security, why doesn't he ban arms sales? We'll do a deal with Reagan: We'll stop exporting cocaine when he stops exporting weapons."

Some people, Tom among them, dismissed the raids as a waste of time. "If America succeeds in keeping out cocaine—and, of course, it never will—some kitchen chemist in New York is going to produce a synthetic equivalent. Now that might reduce the trade deficit, but it won't stop people taking drugs.

"Anyway, knocking out the labs is not the deathblow they think it is. Cocaine doesn't *have* to be processed in Bolivia. There are processing labs in the United States. Miami is full of them. These raids won't finish the drug trade. The most they can do is force it to reorganize."

Over lunch my landlady said Americans wouldn't consume tons of coke every year if they weren't lonely. "Where are the human values in that country?" she asked. "Women are beaten and babies battered. People abandon their parents, and in turn their children abandon them. They care nothing for one another. A telephone in every home, yet no one stays in touch with anyone. America is a cruel place. If I lived there, I'd take drugs too."

The coke industry poses a quandary for the Bolivian government. On the one hand, it regards with genuine concern the growing power of the drug lords and American threats to withhold aid worth some $60 million a year unless they're brought to book. And it worries too that as more and more peasants abandon food crops to grow coca, the country will be forced to buy its food abroad.

But the picture has another side to it. The government is not unaware that coca is now the country's most valuable crop, bringing in far more every year than legal exports. Cocaine revenues keep the country going, and if anything happened to imperil them, the economy would be devastated. In addition, there is the danger of civil unrest. The cocaine industry employs many thousands of peasants, most of them earning several hundred dollars a year. That's more than they've ever made before, and they have warned the government to expect trouble if this income is threatened.

All this had created a delicate situation. Much as the government wanted to rein in the drug lords, it had to do so in a way that neither upset the peasants nor endangered the economy. In the end it took the easy way out: It gave its approval to the lab raids—and then told the drug lords of its decision.

"Those labs were completely deserted," said José when he came to see me in my room that evening. "The Americans expected to make hundreds of arrests. They found no one. Everyone had gone to Panama." He roared with laughter.

"This means, of course, I can't go to Florida," he said, serious now. "This has finished me with America. I'll never set foot in that country again."

He glanced at his watch. "I can't stay," he said. "I just came by to say the offer stands. If you want to run a couple of kilos for me, let me know. And don't worry about the risks. My people will take care of everything."

He stood up.

"That coke you bought last night," he said. "Have you any left?"

"Sorry. It's all gone."

"I thought we'd do a few lines. Never mind. I'll see you around."

He had just left when two policemen arrived. They were polite. They hoped they hadn't come at a bad time. There were a few questions they wanted to ask. Could I spare them five minutes?

"Who is Tom?" the taller of the two began.

"He's someone I chanced on in the plaza. You know as much about him as I do."

"And José? Who is he?"

"A friend of Tom's, I believe. I met him briefly last night."

"He is not a friend of yours?"

"I hardly know him."

"Then what was he doing in your room?"

"He came by to say hello. He stayed a minute or two and left."

"What did you and he talk about last night?"

"It wasn't much of a conversation. We chatted about Chuck Berry for a while. And Janis Joplin. That was about it. Just rock 'n' roll."

The interview was more trying than unnerving, and the police left me with these words: Since it was their job to see that foreigners stayed out of trouble in Santa Cruz, they felt I should know that I was mixing with the wrong people.

There was no demand for money, and no search. Not that they would have found anything. But perhaps they knew that. José may have told them. "That coke you bought last night— Have you any left?"

"I should have warned you this might happen," said the landlady when I told her about my visitors. "Thirty percent of the people in this town are informers. Don't talk to anyone."

"I've begun to wonder if I want to be here at all," I said. "Are there likely to be other interviews?"

"That depends on what people have been telling them. Maybe you should go away for a while. Go to Trinidad for a week. By the time you get back, they'll have forgotten all about you."

I had been planning a trip to Trinidad in any event. An hour by air from Santa Cruz, Trinidad is in the jungle. And jungle was something I'd promised myself in frigid Potosí. "Jungle, jungle, jungle," I would say—over and over—as I tried to forget my freezing feet. The word has something pagan about it. It suggests innocence and nudity, and it made me long to throw off my clothes and lie in the healing sun.

Trinidad is an attractive town, and I was fortunate to be there when it was possible to see it. In the wet season much of Trinidad is underwater. This is why many of its sidewalks are elevated—pedestrians leap onto them like mountain goats— and why too the sidewalks themselves are covered. Unfortunately, neither measure offers much protection from the rain. Flood channels would no doubt help, but the city doesn't have any. A plan to build them was never implemented.

With a population of 40,000, Trinidad is the capital of the Beni and is relatively well-to-do. Its most prominent citizens are cattlemen, its most prominent structure a splendid neo-Gothic cathedral. The cathedral is relatively modern, having been built on the site of a Jesuit church when the latter was destroyed—not by flood waters but by fire—at the end of the last century.

Trinidad is a former Jesuit mission. Starting in 1682 the Jesuits founded fifteen mission-villages in northeastern Bolivia, and into them they gathered thousands of savanna Indians. The Jesuits taught the Indians to weave, to paint, to print, to play music, to raise cattle, and to grow oranges.

Under their tutelage the Indians became accomplished tailors, carpenters, tanners, boat builders, coopers, and joiners. They learned to make clocks and watches. They built their own printing presses. They became master silversmiths. They formed their own string orchestras. They discovered agriculture.

The Jesuits also taught the Indians how to pray, and afterward they were to do little else. They prayed as they marched to work in the mornings; they prayed when they paused for lunch; and when their toil had ended, they prayed as they headed home. They weren't done yet. Back in the mission, they repaired to the church for an hour of hymns, and there were prayers again before they went to bed.

The Indians would seem to have submitted willingly to this twin regimen of work and worship. If their lives had a monastic quality, they were also a good deal less arduous. And considerably more secure. On the savanna the Indians had seen their numbers decimated by slave traders; in the missions they were finally beyond the traders' reach.

For all that, it was often necessary to enforce discipline. The Jesuits created a cadre of children, whose job it was to inform on miscreants. And each mission had its police force, its court of law, and its prison. Penalties ranged from forfeiture of food for those who refused to work to expulsion in cases of recidivism and threats to the mission's security. The majority of crimes involved nothing more serious than drunkenness or sloth, for both of which the punishment was a whipping. Never known to shirk unpleasantness, the Jesuits did their own flogging, usually in public—in the interest of deterrence. Afterward flogger and flogged shook hands—a practice that still survives in many English public schools.

However much the Indians may have looked on the priests as benefactors, Jesuit influence wasn't always benign. When they rounded up their charges, the Jesuits destroyed their culture. They also introduced disease, and the Indians, concentrated as they now were, succumbed to one epidemic after another. Influenza and smallpox alone may have killed as many as 80 percent of them. By 1737, it has been estimated, their numbers had dwindled to fewer than 50,000.

The Jesuits were expelled in 1778. They had been in the Beni—or Mojos, as it was then known—close to a century, and the missions were never more prosperous. Or more resented. The area's other Spanish settlers felt wronged by the Jesuits, whom they accused of depriving them of labor. Moved to act, they persuaded Charles III that the Jesuits meant him harm. The missions had amassed great wealth, the king was told, and posed an implicit challenge to the Crown's authority. Charles had reasons of his own to dislike the Jesuits, and he ordered the fathers seized. Beyond destroying their archives, they offered no resistance.

The missions did not long survive them. Writing in 1939 Gabriel René-Moreno, the Bolivian historian, said that Mojos went into an immediate decline when the Jesuits left. In the 1820s the demand for quinine spurred a revival of sorts, but it was not to last. Cinchonas—the trees from which quinine derives—were soon being grown on plantations in the East Indies. Then came the rubber boom—but this too was short-lived. By 1910 Southeast Asia was producing rubber that was not only cheaper but also more accessible. After that the Beni languished—to rise again in the 1950s. This time cattle provided the stimulus.

I had only one reservation about Trinidad: the surrounding jungle looked tame. I wanted something wild and torrid. Primeval. I appealed to a travel agent.

"If it's authentic jungle you want, I'd suggest La Loma," said this round little man. A birthmark was clearly visible through his thinning hair. "It's three hours from here. You can take a bus."

"It's the real thing?"

"Absolutely!"

"And it's primitive?"

"How primitive do you want?"

"Very primitive."

"It's just what you're looking for."

La Loma has a great air of insouciance about it. I liked it immediately. I had expected a good-sized settlement. I had the idea that a place qualifying for mention on the map would have some mass to it, a substance to distinguish it from its surroundings. In fact, there was nothing. La Loma comprises a few shops widely dispersed along a road going elsewhere. And that is it. We had passed other dispersed shops on the way here. Why those in La Loma would have a name and the others wouldn't is one of the mysteries of modern cartography.

I walked down to the river. The people I asked were unable to name it. "We just call it the river," they said, as if they wondered why *river* wouldn't be name enough. It may be the only river they know. In which case *river* is more than adequate.

Children swam and fished in these languid waters. One of them had a net, another a rod. The latter, standing on the bank, drew up fish after fish. In ten minutes he'd caught six of them. Big ones too. Two of the fish would provide supper for himself and his parents, the boy said. The other four would be given to a restaurant in exchange for milk and bread. Tomorrow he would fish again. He fished every day.

Had he ever failed to catch any?

The idea made him laugh.

"Oh, no," he said. "The river is full of fish."

A boy with warts on his hands was soaping himself in the green water. Farther downstream an old man took off his clothes and washed them. He took his time, working very deliberately. And when he finished, he washed himself. With the same deliberation, at the same slow pace. It was as if this were all he had to do today, and the day's success depended on the thoroughness with which he did it. I imagined him telling his wife over dinner, "A good day, all in all. I got a lot done."

A fish jumped beside him. By now he'd finished bathing, and his clothes had dried.

There was a confidence about all of this that made my heart pound: the confidence of people in their own resources, in nature's beneficence; their confidence that the only obligations they are under are those requiring that they eat and sleep and wash and occasionally procreate.

Over lunch the waiter brought up the subject of drugs. But I refused to be drawn out. The Leopardos—the army's antidrug unit—were in the area. I had seen them patrolling the riverbank: armed to the teeth and wearing a ridiculous quantity of webbing.

Several times they had checked my passport. One soldier, glancing through its pages, wanted to know my nationality. Perhaps it was a trick question.

"I'm Finnish."

"How interesting. According to your passport . . ."

Another asked to see my vaccination card. He held it upside down as he examined it.

"All in order," he said, handing it back. For all he knew, it might have been a shopping list.

I went back to the river after lunch. The jungle comes right down to the water's edge—all of it a thrilling tangle. I picked my way through the trees, many of them in flower. The blooms looked like orchids. In here the light was green and amber—as if it were strained through stained glass. A bird with brilliant yellow tail feathers flew past. A butterfly settled on my arm. In the distance was the sound of falling water. The silence got deeper and deeper, and the air thicker. Finally the day seemed to break under the weight of it all, and it was suddenly dark. A cock crowed. It was six o'clock. Time for supper.

I ventured back to Santa Cruz a few days later. I had an appointment with a former girlfriend. I had gotten to know Sally when I was an altar boy. At mass, when she received communion, I would tickle her chin with the paten. This was rather scandalous, I suppose, but she can't have minded, because one morning she received communion twice—something the church expressly forbids. I took it as proof of her love for me. We were both thirteen at the time, and I was bound to her for the next four years.

Sally and her father rode to church every morning in a pony and trap. Neither looked to left or right. He was said to be very strict. Once, the story went, he had had her whipped. Not wishing to raise his ire, I avoided talking to her. Our only contact was the communion plate.

Her family was known for being aloof. "What they get up to in that house is anybody's guess," I heard someone say once. All anyone knew for certain was that they said the rosary in the evenings. I imagined them as being a little like the Brontës: lots of tuberculosis and religious melancholy.

Her father owned a small dairy farm, and Sally spent her evenings milking cows and churning butter. It struck me later that her early life owed little to the Brontës. It resembled more that of the mission Indians: equal parts work and worship presided over by a parent with a horsewhip.

I had been tickling her chin for nearly a year before I found the courage to talk to her. After that we met every day. She was going to be a nun, she said. It was something her father wanted, and she hesitated to disappoint him. Actually, he would have much preferred that she be a priest, but since that wasn't possible a nun would have to do. Still, she thought she'd find it bearable. She'd go to Africa and work as a missionary. "Those people don't even wear clothes," said this pious little girl. "Imagine: bold as you like, walking around without a stitch. Someone has to civilize them."

And then her sister died tragically, and her family moved away. Quite suddenly and without warning. I was on vacation at the time, and when I got back they'd gone. The house was boarded up, and the trap—sans pony—lay overturned in the garden. What upset me most about this was that we'd recently quarreled. About anchovies, of all things.

"How can you eat those nasty little things?" she'd wanted to know. It was the evening before I was to leave, and we were sharing a pizza.

"They're really quite remarkable," I said. "The anchovy may be little, but it's very, very fierce. It will eat anything small enough for it to swallow. Even its own young."

"That's quite horrible," she said. She knew all about devouring parents. But this was something I realized later. At the time I thought she was being silly, and we parted on bad terms.

I didn't see her again until her family—what was left of it—returned to the area four years later. Her father had recently died, and Sally was free to dispose of her life as she pleased. She didn't become a nun; she became an economist instead. But she retained her missionary zeal. Based in London, she had a job advising foreign governments. This was why she would be spending several days in Santa Cruz. She was preparing a report on ways to develop the Oriente—ways to arrest the decline René-Moreno had attributed to the departure of the Jesuits.

For much of its history, Bolivia has viewed the Oriente, as the lowlands are called, as its last great frontier, its next

Potosi. The region constitutes more than half the national territory, and its potential is vast. Bolivians believe passionately that the Oriente will yet save them—stimulate an economic revival, forge a new national unity. "It's our last hope," they will tell you. "If we could only develop the lowlands, all our problems would be solved."

And if the lowlands aren't developed?

"In that case," many agree, "the country has no future."

Considering the Oriente's importance to Bolivia, one would expect the government to take an interest in it. It doesn't. In 1960, after land reform had depressed food production on the Altiplano, officials unveiled a plan to move more than a million people to the lowlands by the end of the decade. Little came of it. Today 16 percent of the national population lives in the Oriente—a figure little changed in thirty years.

"This country has no interest in the long term," said Sally. "It wants results, but they have to be immediate. I talk to civil servants, and it's the first question they ask: When will we see results? Not for decades, I tell them. And right away, their eyes glaze."

What is needed to develop the lowlands?

"More settlement sites, for one thing. Which means more roads. Right now, there are only three areas to which settlers can move—three areas in which the best land is already under cultivation.

"But the real challenge will be getting people to relocate. As of now, few see the point. Of course they're poor on the Altiplano, they'll tell you; but in the lowlands they'd be no better off. The government has to change this perception, and so far it's failed. Potential settlers would rather look for work in Argentina."

In the absence of small farmers, it is now large landowners who dominate the Oriente. "These people don't need government assistance. They have their own money. They can afford to mechanize; they can hire professional managers; and they aren't plunged into crisis if the harvest is bad. In time, though, they may prove a problem. Without anyone really intending it, the Oriente now has a landed gentry. As the Altiplano did—before the revolution."

Sally wasn't optimistic about Bolivia's prospects. Any more than was Claude, the French journalist with whom we had dinner. But unlike Sally, who believed that Bolivia had to develop more quickly, Claude thought it better that it not develop at all.

"I'm skeptical of the claims being made for growth," he said. "If by growth you mean more consumerism, then I can't see it helping very much. A man with three cars is no better off than the man with one. Too often we make the mistake of confusing poverty and misery. They have little in common."

He ordered a banana split—his second—before resuming.

"The question we should be asking is this: Are the developed countries any better off than the undeveloped ones? I would say they aren't. It's my experience that, far from increasing human happiness, economic growth *reduces* it. By encouraging people to be materialistic, growth makes them less human.

"Consider, if you would, what prosperity has done for our own societies. Can you honestly say that the poor have anything to learn from us? On the contrary: it is we who should be learning from them. Their cultures serve them better than ours do us. Wouldn't it be best, then, to leave them alone?"

"Sanctimonious prig," Sally said later. "Who is he to decide what's best for people? Doesn't he know that Bolivians themselves want higher living standards? What is one to do then? Tell them, ever so gently, that wealth would be their ruin? That it's better to be poor? If he believes that, why isn't he living with them?"

After I left Sally that night, the two policemen interviewed me once again. This time Claude was the focus of their interest. What was he doing here? they wanted to know. Why didn't they ask him themselves? I wondered. Must all their information come from me?

"He's a journalist," I said. "I assume he's gathering material for a story."

But they looked skeptical. My explanation can't have sounded very plausible. Worse, they may have thought I was lying. They became less courteous.

"We'll be keeping an eye on you," said the tall one.

The small one nodded. "We certainly will," he said. "So you'd better watch your step."

I was tired of their warnings. If they didn't want me here, I would oblige them by going. Sally too wanted to leave. Like me, she was interested in learning something about the Chaco War. Though South America's deadliest conflict, it is one that few outside the region know anything about. I wanted to meet the men who'd fought this war. It was out of their disenchantment that the revolution had been born. It was they who had toppled the ancien régime. Those who battled the army in 1952 merely applied the coup de grace.

I wondered if the Chaco veterans liked what they had wrought. Did they consider the new Bolivia any better than the old? To find out, we decided to go to Tarija. Sally had heard that it had a war museum.

It was 1:15 the next afternoon when we took a taxi to the railway station. The train to Yacuiba, I understood, would leave at two.

"Not so," said the taxi driver. "That train left at one o'clock."

Could it be overtaken?

"Perhaps," he said. It made a twenty-minute stop at a station 16 miles away. With luck, we'd catch it there.

We arrived just as the train did. But a policeman stopped us as we tried to board.

"Where are you going?" he asked Sally.

"Yacuiba."

"Yacuiba's in the other direction. This train is going to Brazil."

The Yacuiba train did indeed leave at two. The taxi driver, all apologies now, had assumed we wanted this earlier one.

"Never mind," said the policeman, putting a hand on my shoulder. "I'm heading back to Santa Cruz. The two of you can drive with me."

He proved to be a good sort.

"Those people on the train," he said, "did you see their faces when you got into my car? They thought I was arresting you."

He roared with laughter. And so did I, thanking God, as I did, that my coke had been stolen.

The trip to Yacuiba took fifteen hours, during which our tickets were checked five times and the coca patrol made two brief appearances.

"Do you have any objection to my searching your bag?" I was asked.

"None at all."

"Will you be crossing the border into Argentina?"

"No, we're going to Tarija."

I managed to sleep only a little. The door slammed open and shut all night, and the smell from the toilets was overpowering.

At Villa Montes, where the explorer Jules Crevaux was bludgeoned to death by Indians, a troubadour came on board. He sang several forlorn songs about love gone sour. They were heartbreakingly sad. The train had now stopped in the middle of nowhere, and our car had gone dark. And then the moon came out, flooding the face of this stricken man with light. It was a moment I would long remember.

9

TARIJA was more welcoming than Santa Cruz. Too welcoming, it turned out. Whereas Santa Cruz couldn't wait to see my back, Tarija refused to let us leave.

We had been there five days when the city declared a strike, which would last, it said, until the national government built it a bigger power plant. "This action has been forced on us," said a communiqué from the strike committee. "The government promised to build this plant six years ago. We feel we've waited long enough."

Perhaps they had. But it was hard to be sympathetic. For us the strike couldn't have been more inopportune. We had planned to leave Tarija the next morning, and this was no longer possible. No buses would be running.

Sally best summarized our predicament. "We're fucked," she said.

But not for long, we hoped. An army captain who had traveled from Yacuiba with us seemed to think the strike would be resolved quickly. "Just take my word for it," he said. In the few days we'd known him, it was a phrase he'd used often. That and "I'd say more if my lips weren't sealed." This man worked for military intelligence, he told us, and carried two identification cards, one describing him as an army officer, the other as a student. "Sometimes I'm one; sometimes the other," he said, winking. "It depends on the company I'm in."

Did he think the government would yield and give Tarija its power plant?

"I don't see why it should. If they want a bigger plant, why can't they build it themselves? I'll tell you why: They're lazy. This could be one of the richest towns in Bolivia, but no one wants to work. But, then, who *does* in this country? We'll never develop if we don't change our mentality."

By "we," of course, he meant "they." But it was hard to say what *he* contributed to development efforts—besides disseminating misinformation. Over lunch one day he told us that he had once intercepted a truckload of coca leaves en route to the American ambassador.

"What would the American ambassador want with coca leaves?" Sally asked.

"My lips are sealed on that one," he said.

The next time we ran across him he claimed to have made another interception: this time a planeload of arms intended for left-wing extremists.

"Then congratulations are in order," I said.

"I hardly think so," he said. "Two other shipments may have reached their destination."

"What left-wing extremists are you talking about?" Sally wanted to know.

"Well, I can't be too specific," he said. "Let's just say there are people around here who'd love to bring down the government. If they ever try, there'll be a bloodbath."

"Do you believe any of this?" I asked Sally afterward.

"God, no," she said. "The man's a basket case. Some captain. Captain Fantastic, that's what he is."

Still, I did wonder if he mightn't be a provocateur. In the paper that morning there had been a story about an attack on a local radio station. A bomb had exploded, destroying a transmitter. Both the bishop and local journalists had deplored the incident, the bishop calling it an assault on the integrity of the individual, the journalists taking the view that it signaled a return to the Dark Ages. Both blamed terrorists without suggesting who those terrorists might be. A young worker we met in the post office was less coy. The transmitter had been blown up by people working for the government, he said. Why? Because the station had been critical of the president's economic policies.

"Things are getting worse by the day," he went on. "The government knows it can't control this situation very much longer. That's why it's trying to goad us. It would love an excuse to declare martial law."

"Is the opposition armed?"

"I wish to God we were."

By the next morning much of the city was observing the strike. "Nothing is getting in, and nothing is getting out," our landlady delighted in telling us. "There are barricades on all the main roads. To cross them, you've got to have a letter from the strike committee."

"It looks as if we're stuck," I said to Sally after breakfast. "I suggest we make the best of it."

But she wasn't ready to resign herself. Her flight to London left La Paz in four days, and she still hoped to catch it.

"Let's go down to the bus station," she said. "Perhaps someone there can suggest something."

Someone there—the driver of the bus that would have taken us to La Paz—suggested that we come back that afternoon. "There's a good chance the bus will leave on time," he said, "but I won't know for sure until after lunch. Come and see me about two."

At two we were asked to wait. The bus companies were still in negotiations with the strike committee.

"Keep your fingers crossed," said the driver. "I expect word at any moment."

We waited an hour and a half. And then the decision came down: all buses would be grounded until further notice.

The driver, though, professed optimism. "This thing can't last," he said. "Try us in the morning."

I suspected he was putting off the evil hour when he would have to refund our ticket money.

Sally decided that our only hope was to throw ourselves on the mercy of the strike committee.

"Do you think that's wise?" I asked.

"Why wouldn't it be? They're only people, after all. They can hardly resist an appeal to their decency."

But the committee refused even to hear us.

"There are hundreds of tourists in town," a man at strike headquarters told us. "If we let you go, we'll have to let everyone go. And frankly, that wouldn't be in our interests. The fact that you're here gives us a little leverage."

Then Captain Fantastic turned up again.

"All is not lost," he said, with that knowing air of his. "I've managed to get a car. I'll drive you to Camargo. You can get a bus to La Paz from there."

"And how do you propose to get around the barricade?"

"Easy," he said. "We'll storm it. Let's drive out and take a look."

We drove through a beautiful landscape of golden light, silver eucalyptus trees, and cobbled country lanes until our way was barred by two very large trucks drawn across the road. There could be no thought of storming *them*. But the captain was not discouraged. "This is going to be harder than I thought," he said as we drove back into town. "But never fear; you leave this to me. I'll come up with something. In the meantime, try to enjoy yourselves."

Fortunately, Tarija is an easy place to enjoy. A self-possessed, bustling little town of 60,000 people, it lies in a fertile river valley and supports itself by growing wheat and raising cattle. It also produces its own wine—Arce, Colonial, and Kohlberg. Dreadful stuff, but Sally was upset when I said so.

"Careful," she said. "If we antagonize anyone, we may *never* get out of here."

The ethos here is not Bolivian at all. One might be in Argentina, of which Tarija once formed a part. When Bolivia gained its independence, Tarija sued to join the new republic, taking up arms to press its case. Yet Argentina's influence is as evident as ever here. Spanish is spoken with an Argentine accent, purchases may be paid for with Argentine australes, the menfolk sport a hat long associated with the gaucho, and the music of choice is the tango. With little to bind it to La Paz, Tarija has found itself drawn further and further into the orbit of its neighbor.

Tarija is most fun in the evenings. When the sun sets the *chorizo* sellers appear, their sausages spitting on glowing braziers, the air pungent with the smell of charcoal and garlic and olive oil. And then, a little later, a residential area near the river becomes a huge outdoor restaurant. Women move their gas cookers onto the pavement, while others struggle with chairs and kitchen equipment. Oil lamps are lighted, tables dressed, and menus chalked on front doors. Children are dispatched to buy onions and chilies. And then the cooking begins.

For all its relative remoteness, Tarija has more weltanschauung than either Cochabamba or Santa Cruz. On Mondays newsagents advertised with some excitement the arrival of the latest newsmagazines; and its several bookshops were never less than full. It is also cleaner than those two cities. In the mornings housewives washed down their housefronts or weeded gardens filled with orange trees; in the afternoons children were directed onto peach-tiled roofs to remove offending fungi. The streets were spotless. In the entire time I was there, I saw just one graffito: "Jimy Swagerth [sic] is a scoundrel."

Part of its charm is the feeling that Tarija is a little behind the times, a function, no doubt, of its being far from anywhere. There is something gently old-fashioned about it. The men politely raise their hats to you in the street—so much nicer than the ardor with which one is greeted in the rest of the country. Because even though you know this fervor to be affected, you find yourself after a time greeting others as they greet you, part of you wanting to believe that they are as glad to see you as they appear to be and feeling compelled, in case they are, to appear no less delighted to see them.

The women's fashions too seem a little dated in Tarija— box-pleated skirts and white court shoes. I remembered my mother once having dressed like this. But long ago. Was it twenty years? Twenty-five? These women seem only slightly more contemporary than the Mennonite women in Santa Cruz.

Isolated, Tarija has had to make do, and it has risen to the challenge splendidly. It is now largely self-sufficient, and what resources it has are carefully husbanded. In better-placed communities Tarija's many aging cars would certainly have been discarded. Here, noisy and burning prodigious amounts of oil, they still give service. And in the plaza, with its beautiful cast-iron fountain, portrait photographers crouch behind ancient cameras on ancient tripods.

"Old, aren't they?" an old man asked of this equipment.

"Still, they get the job done." But can they survive much longer? Visiting the plaza two weeks later, I detected a new presence—a man with a Polaroid.

After driving to the barricade with Captain Fantastic, Sally and I took a walk to the university. We had a friend there, a student named Jaime. Jaime's father operated a typing school in the courtyard of our hotel. It was very successful. We woke to the clatter of typewriters, ate to the clatter of typewriters, and at night it was of the clatter of typewriters that we dreamed. That is, if the clatter of typewriters didn't keep us awake.

Jaime was embarrassed by his father's success. "Why couldn't he have been an Indian?" he asked. "Or a worker? It's so unfair. Because I have a bourgeois for a father, my friends refuse to take me seriously."

To establish his radical credentials, Jaime now planned to make what he called "a blood pact with the people."

"Not a *real* blood pact," he explained to us. "There'll be no cutting of thumbs. This will be symbolic."

As for which people he would make this pact with, he wasn't really sure. "It depends on who I can rustle up, I suppose. Anyway, come to the university tomorrow afternoon. We sign the pact at four."

But the signing was deferred.

"It'll have to wait," said Jaime when we met him. "The strike changes everything. This is a direct challenge to the government's authority. It now has no choice. It has to act."

"Act how?"

"Send in troops. Tarija is in revolt. There's only one way to treat a revolt. You crush it. If you don't, it spreads."

"You'd like to see the army take Tarija?"

"Why not? The government would be unmasked. It would have shown its true colors."

The next morning our landlady looked more triumphant than ever. "The city's at a complete standstill," she said. "You'll never get away now."

"Never?"

"They say this is going to last indefinitely. The airport is closed, and the phone lines are down. Tarija is cut off."

Not completely. The strike committee was in telephone contact with La Paz, and there was talk that a government official would visit Tarija in the next few days. To resolve the dispute.

But what would happen if a resolution proved elusive? Would the government then use troops to break the strike, as Jaime had predicted? If it wished, it could easily represent this stoppage as the work of extremists. Or suppose it wasn't the strike that concerned the government as much as the growing opposition to its policies. The administration would love an excuse to declare martial law, the worker had said in the post office. Here, surely, was all the pretext it needed.

As we left the hotel, several trucks filled with soldiers rumbled past. Minutes later they were followed by several more. This—and the small group of whispering men huddled on the corner—convinced me that a general mobilization was under way.

"This looks bad," I said to Sally.

"Yes," she said. "I have this feeling suddenly that I'm John Reed in *Ten Days That Shook the World*."

We walked in the direction of the plaza and came upon six more trucks. They were drawn up outside a church. Several hundred soldiers stood at ease. Each held an aging rifle. There were also numerous military police, looking more fearsome than the soldiers if only because they carried machine guns.

Some twenty soldiers marched to the church door and

formed a gauntlet. An officer shouted an order, and they drew
their truncheons. Good God, I thought, they're going to blud-
geon people as they leave mass.

But it all turned out to be quite innocent: This was Services
Day, and local units of the army and air force had assembled
to honor their patron, Our Lady of Mount Carmel.

In the church people prayed before a statue of San Roque.
One of the petitioners was a Franciscan monk, the skin on
his sandaled feet chapped by cold. In his trim stick-on beard,
San Roque looks quite the young blade. The feathers on the
staff he carries give it the appearance of a Zulu lance. The
saint is a local favorite, having a reputation for being generous
with his favors. When, on his feast day, his statue is carried
through Tarija, women throw him flowers from their balconies.

Mass over, Our Lady of Mount Carmel was borne from
the church on a bier. She was draped in the Bolivian colors.
Someone had pushed a wad of bank notes under her right
foot. Behind her walked the bishop. He wore purple socks
and a purple biretta. The soldiers fell in, marching in step
if not in strict formation. They looked very young. Indians,
all of them. It was people just like them who had been sent
to the Chaco in the 1930s to wage war on Paraguay. Most
of them died of thirst. Two bands—one from the army, the
other from the air force—brought up the rear. The navy
wasn't represented at all; presumably it was fully occupied
guarding Lake Titicaca from the designs of the Soviet fleet.

It was intended that the two bands play in unison. But the
air force struck up before the army was quite ready, and after
several minutes of trying to catch up, the latter lapsed into
sullen silence.

The procession wound around the plaza—once, twice,
three times. The record shop, which had been belting out

tangos ever since we got here, fell mute each time the bier came into view, resuming its transmissions the instant it had passed.

The marchers paused once to let a funeral pass. A miserable thing: a mean hearse followed by a dozen careworn mourners. A single wreath. In the distance, a tolling funeral bell—a sound that never fails to cool my body temperature two or three degrees.

The third time around the plaza, the army was relieved at the bier by the air force. If I might be permitted a generalization, I would say that Bolivian air force officers are shorter than their army colleagues, favor sunglasses, and show a preference for pencil-thin mustaches. They also take more care when they polish their shoes. And, unlike army officers, they carry machine guns. Rifles, presumably, are of little use when fired from airplanes.

Both services looked fairly innocuous, yet these are the people who persistently seize power in this country, turning one democratic government after another out of office. Politically, few countries anywhere can be less stable than Bolivia. Since independence in 1825, it has had sixteen constitutions and over two hundred governments. Which is not so many that it hasn't sometimes found itself with no government at all.

"What the Bolivian armed forces want, the Bolivian people get" is a local adage, the suggestion being that Bolivia is at the mercy of its army. But this is something the military disputes. As it sees things, Bolivia would not exist without it. "We've brought this country back from the brink more times than I can remember," said Captain Fantastic. "If it weren't for us, there wouldn't be a Bolivia. Civilians would have destroyed it."

By the captain's estimation, far from thwarting the democratic process, the military guarantees democracy's survival by ousting governments whose policies threaten anarchy. "The army took power in nineteen sixty-four to save the country from Marxists. If we hadn't intervened, Bolivia would not now have a constitutional government. It would be another Cuba."

It was true, he said, that the army had sometimes nullified elections, but here too its instincts were essentially democratic. These elections, very often, had lacked legitimacy. "You know," he said, "many people won't vote because they don't trust politicians. So you have to ask the question, To what extent does *any* civilian administration reflect the popular will? I'd say, very little."

Are military administrations any different?

"Very much so. The great thing about a military government is that it's above partisan politics. We have one overriding concern: the national interest. A politician asks himself, "Is this policy good for me?" The army wants to know, "Is this policy good for the country?" The difference is patriotism. We put the country first."

Yet the army is not entirely selfless. Like all institutions, it has its interests, and it would be unusual if it didn't pursue them. So although the captain may have been right when he described the country's welfare as the army's first concern, it doesn't surprise that it would see this welfare as being best served by a strong military.

As the army views it, only a strong military can defend the country's borders—something it has never done with very much distinction—and preserve the public peace. Only a strong military can resolve Bolivia's periodic constitutional crises and develop the economy—a crucial concern, this latter, because an expanding economy means bigger military budgets. "I'll be frank with you," said Captain Fantastic. "The barriers to development are so great in this country that a constitutional government is at a disadvantage. What is the army to do in that case? Watch the country languish or undertake that development itself?"

But he was most revealing, perhaps, when he said that the army would never again tolerate a repetition of its treatment after the revolution. "It's hard to believe," he said, "but in the 1950s, the army was virtually disbanded. We'll never let that happen again. Bolivia needs the army. It's the only thing keeping this country together."

The following day was one of hopes suddenly raised and just as suddenly dashed. Word had it for a time that a settlement was imminent, and that the strike was about to end. And then it was said that chances of a settlement had receded, and that the strike would last another week at least. Many were the stories told about the emissary from the government. He was on his way, or he had decided not to come. He was here and talks were proceeding, or talks had broken down and he had returned to La Paz.

Meanwhile there were signs that the strike was faltering. Just before lunch the committee issued a shrill appeal for solidarity. But shortly afterward the mayor urged people to return to work. In the afternoon the Volvo showroom opened for business, and the market was almost back to normal. The Indians, who cook with charcoal and rely on candles for light, had decided that the size of the power plant bore little on their circumstances.

For the moment, the mayor seemed to have the upper hand. But toward evening the strikers struck back. A truck was driven into the plaza, and, as two policemen watched, it was parked so as to block the street completely.

The policemen had it in their power to make the driver move. Or, at the very least, they might have warned approaching traffic. But they chose to do neither, and the driver was allowed to sit in his cab with its picture of the Sacred

Heart as the plaza filled with cars and traffic ground to a halt. He looked hugely pleased with himself. But then, why not? He was, after all, doing what men do best in this country—disrupting.

There was more bad news back at the hotel. The schools had been closed, our landlady now informed us. Several cases of mumps had been detected, and the authorities feared an epidemic. First, *Ten Days That Shook the World*; now, *Death in Venice*.

"I'd make myself comfortable, if I were you," she said. "I'd say you're here for keeps."

We had dinner with Jack and Liz, an Oklahoma couple just arrived from Aguayrenda, a small town eight hours away. (Here we were desperate to get out, and these people had actually bribed their way in.) Liz listened impassively as Jack dwelt on the sexual opportunities afforded by Bolivia.

"In a place like this, it's hard not to be vain if you're blond and blue eyed," he said. But I was left feeling that he had little resisted this assault on his modesty. Liz, he told me later, was simply a traveling companion. They'd been involved for a time, "but when you're traveling, you get so many offers. You'd be crazy not to take advantage of them."

They had been in Aguayrenda to explore Jack's roots. He was distantly related to Alfalfa Bill Murray, who in 1923 had tried to found a colony of yeoman farmers in the area. "No one remembered him," said Jack. "Can you believe that? One of Oklahoma's founding fathers, and no one had even heard of him."

Murray spent nearly six years in Aguayrenda, an area of poor scrubland edged by low hills. The terrain reminded him of his native Oklahoma, he said, and in 1923 he paid the Bolivian government $29,000 to lease 75,000 acres of it. The Tulsa papers called him a utopian, something he vigorously denied. What he was attempting in Bolivia, he said, was no experiment in political extremism. What he hoped to achieve was nothing more radical than a return to the values of the pioneers: a community bound, first and foremost, by the Ten Commandments.

He told prospective colonists that life in Bolivia would not be easy. It would require special qualities. Which was why he sought a special kind of person. He wanted no shopkeepers in his colony. No office workers either. And socialists, especially, were disbarred. For the right people, he said, his experiment offered limitless opportunities. Four years hard work, and every one of them could expect to be rich.

Nearly two hundred people joined him in Bolivia. But less than two years later, all had returned home. Their leaving had been acrimonious. They accused Murray of being tyrannical, of bilking them of money, and of having minimized Bolivia's hardships. He had given them to understand, they said, that Bolivian conditions, while sometimes difficult, did not differ fundamentally from those in Oklahoma. "He didn't tell us about the panthers and the locusts," said one returning colonist, "never mentioned the alligators and tarantulas. And not a word about the scorpions. That's what I couldn't forgive. I hate scorpions!"

Nor were they happy with the teaching facilities and the medical care. There were no schools, and the doctor, they claimed, was addicted to heroin. There was, besides, very little water—a familiar complaint in the Chaco. Who could farm without water?

Murray, who looked a little like Mark Twain, insisted he was glad to see them go. They had lacked mettle, he said, had been disinclined to work. He would find others to replace them—people who shared his pioneering zeal. But his search was cut short. Tensions between Bolivia and Paraguay began to increase, and the Bolivian army drafted his peasant work force. War was brewing. Later his mules were commandeered. And finally the government revoked his lease.

Murray returned to Oklahoma in 1929, arriving just two months before the Great Crash. Suffering from malaria and nursing burns—he had recently fallen into a fire—he was now considerably poorer. His Bolivian adventure had cost him $100,000.

He was elected governor of Oklahoma in 1931. An ardent populist, he spoke of the executive mansion as his ranch and kept a corn patch in the garden. But he was to prove himself as arbitrary a governor as he had been a colonist. He ruled by executive order and used troops to quell his opposition. He had a horror of intellectuals and threatened to outlaw "high-toned bums." Between demagogic outbursts, he found the time to write. *Uncle Sam Needs a Dictator* is one of his efforts. And since no one was more dictatorial than he, he put himself forward for president, running on the slogan "Bread, butter, bacon, beans."

Toward the end of his life, he would speak again of returning to Bolivia. He was disappointed with America—as he had been in 1923. The country had lost its way, he said, when the frontier closed. Industrial barons were the heroes now; the agrarian values of the nineteenth century had been superseded. In Bolivia, though, one might still create America as it had been—a land of resourceful, self-reliant farmers, America as Jefferson imagined it.

He died as he had lived: an anachronism.

Murray chose Bolivia for his colony because of accounts of the place provided by a friend. He may also have read Francis Clark's *The Continent of Opportunity*, published in 1907. Bolivia, wrote Clark, had "resources unequalled by any country of its size in the world," and its future was "commensurate with the heights of its mountains, the depths of its valleys, and the extent of its vast plateaus." In the same year Marie Robinson Wright wrote *Bolivia, the Central Highway of South America*. She did so, she said, because the world had unfairly dismissed this "land of unlimited commercial possibilities." Also in 1907 a Bolivian diplomat told the National Geographic Society that, with a little work and effort, the future greatness of his country was assured. He saw it, he said, becoming "the beacon light of the world, shining with the undimmed brightness of human rights, peace and happiness."

It was customary for descriptions of Bolivia to employ hyperbole. It still is. As recently as 1961 readers of *Bolivia: An Undiscovered Land* were asked to imagine "an earthly paradise where myth and the unknown still exist, . . . a virgin land with everything man could wish for." Much of the literature about Bolivia would convince us that here is a place where man might still create his Eden. It is an attractive notion— one that those with an urge to remake the world have found hard to resist.

Bolivia is unusual in the number of utopians it has attracted—people not in the least deterred that it lacked a government capable of protecting them. That it did was all to the good. Its poor communications and minimal controls merely meant that here they could establish their own centers of authority, their own institutions. In Bolivia, as the Jesuits had been, they would be free to build their ideal commonwealths. Some, like Murray, hoped to revive an old order; others, like Che, to invent a new one. But whether it was the past or the future that inspired them, each brought to Bolivia the same thing: a plan to build a better world.

Unlike Jack, who revered Murray, Liz had little time for him. "Knock, knock, nobody home," she would say whenever the subject came up—as it often did. (Jack saw to that.) "Get my meaning? Or do I have to spell it out?"

Liz had her own reasons for coming to this part of the world. A Seventh-Day Adventist, she was making a pilgrimage to Cotagaita, the town, not too far from here, in which Bolivia's first Protestant martyr had died. "He was stoned to death by two Indians," Liz said. "A terrible thing. And when he was dead, they tied him to a rock and threw his body in the river."

"Were they ever punished?"

"You might say they were," she said, grinning. "The police refused to arrest them, but a month later one was kicked in the head by a mule, and the other was struck by lightning."

A legal secretary, Liz hoped to be a missionary one day herself. "I want to work right here," she said. "I thought of going to India, but it gets too hot. Anyway, there's more work to do here. It's been neglected."

But that is changing. Bolivia has a growing Protestant presence. Adventists, Mormons, Baptists, Pentecostals—all are making a determined effort to win recruits. To the increasing chagrin of the Catholic church, which accuses them of sheep rustling, Protestants now claim to make thousands of conversions every month.

Protestant missionaries reached Bolivia in the 1880s, and their first converts were a young brother and sister. The children made decisions for Christ, wrote Francis Penzotti, the nineteenth-century colporteur, and "the hovel [in which they lived] became a center of light."

The Adventists are now the country's biggest Protestant denomination, said Liz. "There are days when we baptize up to two thousand people."

The strike might have been winding down, but it was far from over. Many shops remained closed, and shortages had developed. Early in the week our landlady had removed our linen table napkins and replaced them with the paper kind.

"Just a precaution," she said. "I want to conserve my washing powder."

But now the paper napkins too had disappeared. She had exhausted her supply.

There was worse to come the next morning. There were no *salteñas* for breakfast. "I've looked everywhere," she said. "You can't get flour for love or money."

The two Bolivian students who ate at our table were aghast. "But I always have *salteñas* in the morning," said the one who had recently read *Wuthering Heights*. He had identified with Heathcliff, he told me.

"You'll have to manage without them," said the landlady. "We must all learn to make sacrifices."

They contented themselves with arm wrestling. It was all they ever seemed to do. They arm-wrestled through breakfast, lunch, and dinner. Every day. We were careful not to pay them much attention—difficult when their exertions threatened to overturn the table. When conscious of being observed, their wrestling became ferocious. Watch them long enough, I didn't doubt, and one or the other would have his arm wrenched out.

Leaving Tarija had become the sole topic of conversation, an obsession. Flights, taxis, buses, barricades, appeals to the strike committee, appeals to the mayor—it was all anyone talked about anymore. People had begun to look fatigued, no one more so than the German woman who had to return to Hamburg the next week but who still hoped to see Machu Picchu.

She'd had nothing but trouble. Her flight from Buenos Aires to La Paz was canceled when Aerolíneas Argentinas fired all its pilots. She took a bus to Tarija instead. "I thought I could fly to La Paz from here," she said. "Imagine my surprise."

Then yesterday she'd heard of a man who owned a small plane. He would fly her to La Paz for $300, he said. It was an astronomical sum, and more than she could afford. Still, Machu Picchu is Machu Picchu. And it wasn't as if she'd be in South America again. But at the airport, another disappointment. The price of her seat had doubled, and she had to yield her place to someone else.

Several more shops opened this morning, but this only increased the uncertainty. Events were now taking their own course, and no one—not even the chairman of the strike committee—could predict what would happen next. This made it very hard to do anything. The bus station had to be visited in the morning and again in the afternoon in case there were developments. And an ear had to be kept to the radio for the latest communiqué from the strikers. Every hour, on the hour, we tuned in. But they were always the same: "Tarija is now more resolved than ever. . . . The government has ignored us long enough . . . broken promises . . . the future of our children . . . no surrender."

I spent the morning in the museum—and remembered why we had come to Tarija. Besides a portion of a *Cuvieronius Andium*—a predecessor of the elephant—it contained a number of Chaco War remnants: some photographs, a bandolier, holsters, and a grenade case. During the war's later stages, Paraguay had briefly occupied Tarija. Many people died. A memorial to them stands by the river: a soldier marching, his bayonet raised. The posture is defiant, but the expression on his face is one of abject terror.

I'd seen other memorials in other places. In Quillacollo, near Cochabamba, a soldier, half-dead of thirst, pulls himself forward on his stomach. In Vallegrande a simple plaque commemorates the deaths of the four Aramayo brothers. In Sucre, Oruro, Potosí. . . . There isn't a community in this country the war hasn't touched.

In La Paz I'd attended a mass for Chaco veterans. Old men now, most of them white haired. They wore tattered war decorations on their chests. Several of them cried. There were war widows there too. Aymara women all in black. One of them, bereaved some fifty years, was so upset by it all her friends had to help her from the church.

After mass veterans and widows marched through La Paz, preceded by an army band. The widows had been given Bolivia's colors to carry—a piece of bunting 100 feet long. There was not enough of it to go around, and scuffles broke out as the widows vied for the honor of bearing it. The victors removed their hats, a measure of the solemnity they attached to the occasion.

Until the 1920s Paraguay had held most of the Chaco for as long as anyone could remember. Although the border between it and Bolivia had never been precisely drawn, La Paz seemed to accept the Paraguayan presence. True, Bolivia maintained a token force in the area. For the most part, though, it viewed the Chaco much as it did its other frontiers: It had no special value that the government could see, and it was, besides, far away.

The country had a change of heart when this area of arid desert was discovered to have large reserves of oil. But quite possibly little would have come of this either—had President Daniel Salamanca not needed to deflect attention from the tottering Bolivian economy. Then, in 1932, Paraguay seized a Bolivian fort in the Chaco. Actually the fort belonged to Paraguay and had been seized by Bolivia six weeks earlier. But this was of no account. Salamanca, a man much in the Melgarejo mold, had been provided with his casus belli, and he formally announced that Bolivia and its neighbor were now at war.

Bolivia would lose this war—the biggest and bloodiest in South America's history. Some 90,000 people died, two-thirds of them Bolivians. Salamanca had underestimated Paraguay's resolve as well as his own preparedness. Although his army was larger and more sophisticated, the Bolivian high command was to prove shockingly inept. In the field senior officers showed themselves to know little of either strategy or logistics, and many thousands of their men died as a consequence.

Most of the Bolivian dead were Altiplano Indians, people with no experience of the tropics. To reach the front they had to journey 1,000 miles by train and truck, then 500 more by mule and on foot. In the Chaco, with their supply lines overextended, they were expected to fight a war although they had neither arms nor medical supplies, water nor food. Many died without ever seeing the opposing side. The Chaco, and their own officers, proved the greater enemy.

Conditions were appalling. In addition to hunger and thirst, the Bolivians had to fight rodents and rattlesnakes, tarantulas and panthers, swarming flies, and insects that penetrated the foot and made walking impossible. Hazards to which the Paraguayans—with their greater experience of the area—were long accustomed, claimed Bolivians by the thousand. It has been estimated that more died of thirst and disease than ever fell in battle.

In the end the two sides exhausted each other, and peace was declared on June 14, 1935, at 2:00 P.M. A Bolivian named Martín Tudela was killed by a rifle shot a minute earlier. He was the Chaco War's last casualty—a distinction he is unlikely to have sought.

The war was to change the course of Bolivia's history. In the Chaco, Bolivians found their senior officers to be corrupt and venal and tragically stupid. It was not a happy discovery. These officers, supposedly, were Bolivia's best and brightest. Why had they proved so inadequate? What had gone wrong? And why was this war being fought at all? For the first time, the capacity of Bolivia's ruling class was being seriously ques-

tioned. A process had been initiated that in time would cul-
minate in the revolution of 1952.

In Tarija I met numerous people who had fought in that
war. One was a photographer, a man I'd seen fuss with one
of those ancient cameras in the plaza. In his seventies, he
was now half blind. Poor eyesight made him slow. By the
time he was ready to take his pictures, it often happened that
his subject had wandered away.

"We weren't fighting the Paraguayans," he told me. "We
were fighting the desert and the heat. We were fighting only
to survive. When I think about it, I can still taste the dust,
still feel my tongue swell. We had one thought: water. There
was never enough of it. We lacked bread and sugar too. But
that didn't matter. For a little water, I'd have renounced food
forever. We fought for water. We killed for it."

He said he was so thirsty that he would suck the water
out of mud. Once he had slit the veins of a dead man and
drunk his blood. "You flinch," he said. "But a thirsty man
will do anything."

Another time, when a colleague seemed about to die of
thirst, he had offered him his urine.

"Did he drink it?"

"He drank it all right. He was glad to get it. It saved his
life."

Many men drank their own urine, he said. "But most of
the time our bladders were empty. We were so dehydrated,
we couldn't even cry. When we tried, no tears came.

"It rarely rained. But when it did, what joy! We'd lie on
our backs with our mouths open and drink. Drink and drink
and drink. I've never known pleasure like it."

He and his comrades spent the war digging for water. "All
we had were our tin plates. But we dug anyway. Sometimes
as deep as a hundred feet. I remember one well especially.
We dug for months and found nothing. But we wouldn't stop.

One more foot, we'd say. Let's dig one more foot. We'd been digging six weeks when the Paraguayans attacked. They wanted water too. But we drove them back. We'd have fought to the last man to keep that well. And nothing in it.

"Thirst killed many of my closest friends. Others choked to death on dust. I can still see them: men shriveled to half their normal size, youngsters grown old overnight. They lay in the sand with their mouths open. Even dead, they craved water."

Once, he said, a man—badly wounded and crazed by thirst—begged him to kill him. "He was dying and in terrible pain. We had no medical supplies, and his leg and arm were gangrenous. Maggots everywhere. He'd have been better off dead. But I couldn't bring myself to do it.

"Later that day, we found four of our soldiers. They'd been decapitated. Their heads had been neatly arranged—each forming the corner of a square.

"Horrible? I suppose so. We hardly noticed. Most of the time, we were barely alive. We prayed for death, prayed to be taken prisoner. More than ten thousand of us deserted. Can you wonder? The Paraguayans hated us, beat us all the time. We didn't mind. They had water. It was worth being beaten for. I enjoyed being a prisoner. Once, a Paraguayan gave me an orange. I kept it in my pocket for months."

As a prisoner, he was also safe from rats. "In the desert, rats were everywhere. They were drawn by our food. There were so many. In the end, we learned to coexist with them. We gave them part of our rations. If we hadn't, they would have eaten us. They were fat and thick—healthier than we were. At night they'd run across our chests. They were fearless. In some units if you killed ten rats, you'd get more rations. I heard of one man who doused them in gasoline and set them on fire. He liked to hear them scream."

He seemed about to cry.

"But some good came of it," I said. I hoped to sound encouraging.

"Of what?" he asked.

"The war. Without the war, there wouldn't have been the revolution."

"Oh, that. Yes, the revolution made a big difference. Before the revolution, we were poor. Now, we're destitute. The revolution destroyed the one source of income this country had—mining. The revolution ruined us."

"You see no gains at all?"

"No gains worth ninety thousand lives. No gains worth one life. And I'll tell you something else. There isn't a veteran in this town who doesn't agree with me."

Solemn music issued from the record shop on the plaza all the next morning. But after lunch it was playing tangos again. The noon communiqué had contained some good news. The government's emissary had arrived, and talks were scheduled to begin in two days. In the meantime the committee, to show its goodwill, was suspending the strike.

Any relief we may have felt was allayed by another communiqué an hour later: The committee wanted to stress that its deciding to suspend the strike was not a capitulation, and the government shouldn't see it as such. If the upcoming talks failed to make what the committee considered reasonable progress, the strike would resume immediately.

Our course was now clear to us.

"Don't hang around," people told one another. "Tomorrow may be too late. Get out while you can."

Which is precisely what most people did. Taxis did a roaring trade, the airline office was chockablock, and hundreds of people jammed the bus station.

The committee's decision caught the bus lines napping: service wouldn't be resumed until late the next day. In the meantime we tried to book seats on a flight the next morning to Sucre. Again, nothing was certain.

"It depends, señor," said the reservations clerk.

"On what?" I asked.

"It depends," he said again.

The next morning we succeeded in getting a single seat. Sally, we decided, should be the one to have it. Unlike me, she was pressed for time. I would stay in Tarija one day more and then fly to La Paz. There I'd take a bus to Copacabana, on Lake Titicaca. Carnival was about to start. Before leaving for home, I wanted to see Bolivia *en fête* again.

I had my last lunch in Tarija with Jack and Liz. We ordered *saici*, a kind of roast-beef hash. None of us enjoyed it very much. My companions were bickering, and conversation was difficult. And then Jack mentioned Butch Cassidy and the Sundance Kid. Hadn't they lived in this part of Bolivia? What ever became of them?

I'd just finished reading *Across South America*, the book Hiram Bingham wrote in 1911, and had my own theory on the subject. Bingham told of *yanqui* outlaws being gunned down by Bolivian soldiers in a hut outside Tupiza, a town not very far from where we were lunching. The outlaws, whom Bingham didn't name, had been run out of the American West by Pinkerton agents, he said; and they'd met their end while attempting a payroll robbery.

After confiscating the outlaws' mules, the soldiers made Bingham a present of one. "He turned out to be a wonderfully fine saddle mule," Bingham wrote.

Although controversy surrounds the fate of Cassidy and his sidekick, Bingham's story largely coincides with Pinkerton's account of their demise. According to the agency, the two outlaws were killed in a hut near San Vicente by a detachment of Bolivian cavalry investigating a robbery. The soldiers had been directed to the hut by police who had gone there to question its occupants about a mule in their possession. The year was 1911.

True, the two accounts differ as to where, precisely, the killings occurred. But Tupiza and San Vicente are not far apart, and a hut near one might be described just as accurately as a hut near the other. It seems not unlikely then that the "wonderfully fine saddle mule" the soldiers gave Bingham had once belonged to Cassidy.

Bingham became very fond of this animal, riding it through Bolivia and across the Andes into Peru, where a few months later he discovered the lost Inca city of Machu Picchu. What became of the mule after Machu Picchu? We don't know. We may be confident, though, that it avoided the fate of Chico, that other mule which, half a century later, would provide Che Guevara with several steak dinners. That was something Bingham would never have allowed.

10

I N C O P A C A B A N A , our efforts to cross Lake Titicaca to the Island of the Sun were hindered by the navy. The boat-man who had contracted to take ten of us for a total of forty dollars balked when we tried to board his craft. His boat could hold a maximum of six, he told us now. "I'm sorry," he said. "But I have to think of your safety."

At first we took this display of scruple simply to mean that he wanted more money. But our offer of a further twenty dollars was rejected. "I can take six of you and no more," he said, glancing at the naval station, where several sailors were watching us through binoculars. "That's all the law allows."

We walked along the beach until we were out of the sailors' range of vision and found another boatman. This one proved only slightly less cautious, making us sneak on board with the stealth of pirates and crouch below the gunwale until Copacabana was far behind.

The others in our party were three Indian women, a French widow, and five Argentines. Nice people, the Argentines. All mention of the Falklands and the recent England- Argentina soccer match was scrupulously avoided. I appreciated their delicacy, but it had the effect of making all of us self-conscious. One of them, at a loss for something to say, inquired suddenly if I was a Catholic.

"Ah," she said when I told her that I wasn't. The tone was intended to imply that, Catholic or not, it was all the same to her. Yet I was left feeling that my answer had disappointed her. After that she gave up on me, and the conversation languished.

The widow was called Michele, and I began by being delighted by her. Three years earlier her husband had died, and Michele had embarked on what she called a new life. This was very admirable, of course. Unfortunately, she thought so too, and it made her sanctimonious. She took a special delight in describing the response of her friends when she decided to move to Bolivia.

"They told me I was mad," she would say, laughing. "But it's good to be mad, no?"

Since leaving France she had made several discoveries, she said. Society, she realized now, is a prison; schools are nothing more than training camps; and marriage is a medieval survival that has long outlived its usefulness. I heard her enunciate these ideas several times, and always when she did her pupils would dilate and sweat would form on her upper lip. This woman found herself enchanting.

She was particularly vain about her age. "How old do you think I am?" she would ask people within moments of meeting them. And then would answer the question herself. "Fifty-four," she would announce. "Not bad, yes?"

One never knew quite what to say to this. Fifty-four, after all, is not so remarkable an age. One quite often meets people in their fifties—people no less vigorous than she and possessing no fewer faculties. Why would she think she was due some special credit?

She would preach to anyone who would listen. Crossing the lake now, she gathered the Indians around her and expatiated on the dignity of deprivation. They mightn't know it, said this woman of comfortable means, but they were very lucky to be poor. They nodded in solemn agreement, their eyes, as they did so, fixed on her Cartier watch.

"Besides, you have this," she said, gesturing toward Titicaca's cobalt waters. The lake is almost 1,000 feet deep here and stretches as far as the horizon. "The highest lake of its size anywhere in the world! What more could you want?"

The journey to the Island of the Sun took almost three hours, and when we got there, we were delayed again. One of the Indians had a lot of baggage—far more than anyone else—and the boatman demanded that she pay a surcharge. She demurred, saying that she always traveled with these bags for precisely the amount she'd given him. And what was more, she went on, she wouldn't pay another peso. But the boatman was equally adamant. Unless she coughed up, he said, he would impound her luggage. And to prove he meant it, he threw one of her sacks into the hold.

At this the woman went berserk, babbling Spanish and Aymara and clinging first to the boatman and then, when he pried himself loose, to the door of his cabin. I expected the two other Indians to intervene on her behalf. Instead, they demanded that she compose herself. And then, when she seemed about to force her way into the hold (with the intention, I suppose, of retrieving her property), the bigger of the two—a massive person—settled the matter by barring her way. The case was now shut, and the disputant withdrew.

According to the boatman, who was not terribly communicative, some two thousand people live on the Island of the Sun, and all of them, it was my impression, turned out for our arrival. Some requested money, while others wanted to be photographed—for a consideration. They were not especially photogenic. They wore full Aymara attire, yet they seemed not to care how they looked. Their derbies were battered, their shawls soiled, their blouses torn. Even the colors, normally splendid, looked wan: the reds gone to pink, the purples now pale blue. One of the Argentines agreed to pay the price asked of him if the teenage model first changed her skirt.

"What's the matter with this one?" she wanted to know.

"It needs a good wash," he said.

The island, from a distance, had the appearance of a great yellow hump. On closer inspection, it proved to be terraced: long, lateral lines skirt its flanks and make it look like a head of plaited hair. Legend has it that the sun was born here. "The Indians say . . . that for many days the world was in darkness, and while they were all in blackness and obscurity, there rose from this island . . . a resplendent sun," Pedro de Cieza de León, Spain's soldier-historian, wrote in 1553. "For this reason, [the Indians] hold the isle to be a sacred place."

It's also beautiful, and I should have liked the chance to wander around by myself. In this company I felt constrained. I didn't dare look too rapturous for fear of appearing the "sensitive soul" so often dismissed as insincere—or disliked for his lack of inhibition.

Michele, though, had no such scruples. "How exquisite," she exclaimed over this and that—always something one had seen oneself minutes earlier. I think she imagined that, without her to point it out, we'd fail to notice the beauty around us. Fortunately, there were lots of steps to climb—the Inca passion for stairs is an aspect of their psychology still to be investigated—and soon she was puffing like a steam engine: too winded to wax rhapsodic.

I shouldn't have, but I let Michele talk me into spending the night on the island with her. An acquaintance had given her the address of friends. I had misgivings about arriving at dusk, since doing so gave these people little choice but to put us up—and feed us besides. But Michele was convinced they'd be happy to see us. As it happened, the friends were in Copacabana, leaving us with the problem of finding accommodation on an island with neither hotel nor restaurant. It was now, to boot, quite dark and getting colder by the minute. And there wouldn't be a boat till morning.

After much bounding over crevices and traipsing across newly turned earth, we found a young Indian—Manuel—prepared to provide us with room and board. "But you'll have to pay something," he said.

His one-room house was built of mud bricks. To keep out drafts, the inside walls were lined with sheets of newspaper. (One of them bore the headline "The Casuistry of Pascal.") Plastic sheeting reinforced the ceiling.

An occasional miner, Manuel lived alone. Yet oddly enough he owned two double beds. His only other furniture was a small gas cooker and a battery-operated record player.

Light was provided by a candle. But we didn't need it. The moon had risen. A full moon. It was almost as bright as day. In this semilight the island's scattered vegetation looked like a series of inkblot tests. In the distance a fire flared.

Michele caviled when Manuel produced our dinner—potatoes and eggs. Surely he could come up with something better, she told him. She hadn't eaten all day. But it was all he had, and when she complained of still being hungry when she'd finished, I passed her my plate.

She was further aggrieved when told that she and I would have to share a bed. "We've only just met," she told Manuel. She sounded quite the bourgeois.

"Then one of you can sleep on the floor," he said reasonably.

Michele looked at me. I looked at the ceiling. I would not let her bully me.

"Very well, then," she said. "But I must insist you wear your clothes."

"You left the door open," she told Manuel the next morning. "Our bags might have been stolen."

He looked startled. "Nobody steals anything here," he said.

He was startled again when we asked if we might return to Copacabana on one of Titicaca's reed boats.

"You want to drown?" he wanted to know.

"But they're tough and buoyant," I said. "Thor Heyerdahl sailed from Africa to America in one."

"So I've heard," he said skeptically.

Michele rolled her eyes. "See how we've corrupted these people? A boat is no longer a boat unless it has an outboard motor!"

Michele's payment to Manuel for putting her up was a flask—certainly useful and something which genuinely pleased him—and a set of crayons. The latter were more important than the flask, she told him, because "each of us has been given the gift of creativity. . . . It isn't necessary to draw well; it is necessary only that one draw."

She suggested that he have his friends over for drawing parties.

Manuel glanced around his home, with its newspapered walls and its hard-packed floor. "Maybe I will," he said. And put the crayons in a drawer.

My hotel in Copacabana was on a street of modest restaurants all advertising the same lunch—*picante de pollo*—at the same price. I was at a loss to understand why some should be full and others deserted. The busier ones also drew pigs. In hopes of being thrown a morsel, they would stand by the door and try to look winning. When they seemed about to venture in, the restaurateurs would rush at them, pretending to pelt them with stones.

A place of worship since Inca times, Copacabana continues to be South America's holiest shrine. Its largest structure is the cathedral housing the Dark Virgin of the Lake, Bolivia's patron saint. The figure is the work of a sixteenth-century Indian sculptor, and numerous miracles have been attributed to it. It is said to draw pilgrims from many parts of the world.

If I strained, I could see the cathedral from my hotel room. In addition to being small, this room was invariably cold. Located in the building's farthest recess, it got so little sunlight that one might have been living far underground. Three months ago I would have complained. Now I could enjoy it. There was something in my nature, I was discovering, that relished discomfort.

An odd place, this hotel. "Carry out your own dead," said a sign in the lobby. I took it for a joke. But that was before I saw the profusion of electrical wiring in my bathroom. When the hotel was modernized, the owner balked at the cost of concealing the wiring in the walls. For a person brought up to fear electricity, it was a constant source of terror. I took less and less time over my ablutions.

I ate most of my meals in the market, a place popular with schoolboys because many of the vendors sold women's underwear: corsets and knickers were piled high everywhere one looked. The boys could scarcely believe their eyes, and it always happened when I was there that one of them, bolder than the others, would fit a bra across his chest while his fellows shrieked with horror.

It was over just such an incident that I saw two youngsters come to blows. One had begun to try on a bra when the other punched him in the nose. Maybe he thought that women were being besmirched. This minor scrimmage drew a crowd of forty people, suggesting perhaps that Copacabana lacks for entertainment. Highly appreciative they were too, urging on their young champions with shouts of "keep your fists up"; "don't expose your stomach"; and "go for the chin."

"What's going on?" a man asked me.

"I believe they're fighting over a bra," I said.

If this seemed an odd explanation, Brad affected not to notice. A New Yorker, he was in Copacabana for Carnival, a seventy-two-hour revel scheduled to start in two days' time. It promised to be fun. An Indian affair, it is by most accounts the most boisterous event in the Bolivian calendar.

Brad was amiable, and he and I drank Singani, that noxious white spirit, late into the night. I felt awful the next morning. My head felt as if someone were sitting on it. After a queasy breakfast of greasy eggs, Brad suggested we take a walk.

"Good idea," I said, thinking he meant a short stroll around the town. In fact, our little trek would last eight grueling hours and become, for me, a kind of Calvary.

We set out along the lakeshore, passing some of the richest farmland in Bolivia. A beautiful landscape, but I saw little of it. I got progressively sicker.

"I really should go back," I said. "I'm feeling very weak."

"That's why I got you out here," said Brad. "You need air, exercise."

What I really needed was to lie very still. But I struggled on as best I could. And then my head began to swim.

"I can't take another step," I said. "I think I may collapse."

What I did was much more shameful: I threw up—just as Brad was explaining how totalitarian states differ from authoritarian regimes.

He was now more resolved than ever to press ahead.

"We have to get you a stiff drink," he said. "If we keep going, we're sure to find a bar."

I was ill enough to agree to anything.

"Let's try over there," I said, pointing to a distant huddle of cottages.

But the houses, when we reached them, were all empty. A deserted village. And beyond it, a cemetery gone to seed.

Brad seated himself on a tombstone, which promptly crumbled under him. "Where do you think everyone's gone?" he said, leaping to his feet.

"Maybe they were fleeing the lake. I understand its waters rise. It's very high right now."

"That's possible, I suppose. Or they may be looking for work in La Paz. Or Chile. Or Argentina. Did you know there are a million Bolivians in Argentina alone? Everyone I've met here wants to leave. I've talked to people who want to move to New York. You won't get more desperate than that." He shook his head.

"Though I can't say I blame them," he said. "I wouldn't want to live in a country with so dubious a future. Look at it! Abandoned houses and a decaying graveyard. It's not a country at all."

Carnival began the next day with a parade. Banners identified the participants—fishermen, florists, and kiosk owners. They all looked very serious: half embarrassed, half proud. Each carried a Bolivian flag, and one woman was taken to task for failing to hold hers at the proper height. There was also a contingent of schoolchildren. Very young, they made a bad job of marching in formation, and their teachers, women in crushed-velvet skirts, darted among them, pulling them into line.

The reviewing party on the steps of the alcaldía comprised city and provincial officials as well as two officers from both the army and the navy. The army officers wore gloves.

The keynote speech was an all-purpose thing: much like last year's, I suspected, and much like next year's too no doubt. Bolivians were urged to remember that the work of Bolívar and Sucre had still to be completed; much remained to be done; great effort was called for as well as great discipline; everyone would be asked to make sacrifices; the country would have to pull together; et cetera, et cetera, et cetera.

The speaker also served notice on Bolivia's neighbors that the country would continue to agitate for a port on the Pacific. This clearly pleased the naval officers, who were seen to square their shoulders. They squared them again when ten children issued from the alcaldía, one representing each of Bolivia's nine departments, the tenth symbolizing the territory lost to Chile more than a century ago.

This last figure—a little girl—was dressed entirely in black. Her face covered, she walked with her head bowed, her hands chained behind her back, and her feet manacled. She brought to mind those penitential figures who took to the streets in colonial Potosí in the hope of staying the wrath of God. At the sight of her, the reviewing party broke into patriotic song, and there were numerous shouts of "Viva Bolivia." And then the crowd dispersed. The parade was over.

Copacabana's population had doubled overnight. There were tourists everywhere, and more arrived by the hour. They were easy to recognize. They flinched when touched. Many wore poorly made alpaca sweaters—purchased in the belief they were getting bargains.

There were thousands of Indians in town too. Many had come to visit the Chapel of the Candles, a long, windowless vault next to the cathedral. Its only furnishings were three stone tables, on which supplicants set lighted candles, usually six but sometimes as many as two dozen—the exact number determined by the nature and gravity of the request.

At one point there must have been as many as several hundred candles burning in this sepulchral place, and the effect was stunning. Lit like this, the Indians look extraordinarily ancient. Fantastic shapes leapt on the ceiling. And on the walls, petitioners had used molten wax to fashion houses and cars. It was for these they prayed.

Some people chatted happily as they set up their candles. Others looked solemn, their eyes screwed tight. A woman began to chant something, and an old man—half blind, although in this light it hardly mattered—stumbled in with a crucifix so big it towered over him. He was one of those indigents who will pray on your behalf if you give him alms. The crowd cleared a path for him, and a child kissed his hand. It was all quite lovely.

By nightfall Copacabana was drunk to a man, and it would stay that way for the next day and a half. Drink was pressed on one everywhere one went. Everyone, it seemed, carried a bottle of Singani, and all were in a mood to share.

All this made for camaraderie. I had my hand wrung and my back slapped by people I had never seen before. One man—much inebriated—cried at the pleasure of seeing me. Another—an acquaintance of some five minutes—said I was unquestionably the most genial person he had ever met. He too was intoxicated.

This last fellow had a rose in his buttonhole. He was going to a wedding, he said. Since he could hardly stand, I asked if he shouldn't rest a little first. "Turn up like this and you may embarrass the groom," I said, remembering my own calamitous wedding.

"Not likely," he said. "I *am* the groom."

Besides, he was not to be married until the next morning; in the meantime he meant to live it up. An aunt of his was giving a party. And since he was now more convinced than ever of my geniality, he was going to insist, he said, that I come along.

He'd forgotten his relative's address. But he'd know the place when he saw it. "We'll find it soon enough," he said. "Copacabana is not La Paz."

But for all the luck we had, it might have been. Two hours' hunting yielded nothing, although I doubt that our search was very systematic. I seem to recall returning again and again to a street with a hole in it. I remember the hole particularly because it was very large, and I kept falling into it.

The only excuse I can offer is that I was by now very, very tired. This is why I hate Singani. I have only to drink a bottle of it, and right away I feel exhausted. And it doesn't affect only me like this. My companion was feeling no less weary. It was more than either of us could do to stay on our feet.

The groom became so tired, finally, that he was forced to take a nap. All this walking had worn him out, he said, sinking to his knees. If his memory served him, his aunt lived just around the corner. But first he'd have to catch his breath. Ten minutes sleep. Five, even. And then we could resume.

"You can't sleep here," I said. "You'll catch cold."

I wasn't to worry, he said. He often slept out-of-doors. On this very street, if he wasn't mistaken. Although he was sure I wouldn't mind if he were . . . He was so weary, he could hardly think anymore. . . . Besides, I was very genial. . . . His aunt's party . . . And anyway . . .

He was sound asleep.

I left him in a doorway looking much the worse for wear. Mud caked his face—and his suit was torn at the knee. On top of which his rose was missing. I hate to imagine the figure he must have cut when he made it to the altar.

For the rest of the night, Copacabana shook to the sound of firecrackers. Several dozen at least exploded right below my window. It felt as if the hotel had come under heavy bombardment. I didn't get a wink of sleep. I pretended not to mind. But that's hard to do when you've slept badly the night before, and the night before that; harder still when something tells you that tomorrow night will be no less noisy than this one, and you won't sleep then either.

There were more firecrackers in the plaza the next morning. And a fireworks display—flaring catherine wheels and rockets spewing lots of colored smoke. They made an awful racket and terrified both dogs and children. One little boy was alarmed enough to scuttle under his mother's skirts. She reached down and drew him out as if she were an obstetrician. Perhaps recalling a similar emergence on another occasion, he screamed lustily.

Groups of drunk musicians wandered the streets, stopping to play when the fancy took them. These impromptus became increasingly erratic. They'd play briefly and then stop for refreshments. A glass of Singani would be passed around, replenished from those gallon cans in which gasoline is sold. Perhaps they thought that if they drank a little more, they'd play a little better; or it may have struck them that if they could play at all, they couldn't have drunk nearly enough. Play would resume and be followed by another break. Play, break; play, break . . . until the stage was reached when they no longer cared to play. As often happens when people refresh themselves too assiduously, they wanted now only to sleep.

To distinguish one group from another, members of each dressed alike. With time, however, these distinctions broke down. Musicians separated from their fellows attached themselves to the first band that chanced along. Men in tan trousers and orange shirts now cropped up in groups attired in black and white; men in green and beige infiltrated the ranks of the red and blue; and brown and yellow stood shoulder to shoulder with pink and gray.

One such motley crew disrupted a rare public appearance by the Dark Virgin of the Lake. Followed by an entourage of priests, sacristans with candles and censers, and children dressed as nuns and monks, the Virgin was being borne around the plaza on the shoulders of sixteen groaning men. All went well until the procession reached the alcaldía, where it was noticed by a brass band; no doubt intending to pay its respects, the band fell in behind and struck up the national anthem.

As the music got louder and louder, the sacristans, who may only have wanted to escape the din, quickened their pace, which forced the priests to quicken theirs. The fathers were now trotting. This disconcerted the litter bearers. Priests *don't* trot, after all. Not usually, anyway. Something had to be amiss. Now thoroughly alarmed, the litter bearers began to run, their precious cargo wobbling above them as they did so. Normally, the Virgin makes several sedate rounds of the plaza when she ventures out. On this occasion, she was whisked back to her shrine with enough haste to make her head spin.

At dinner that night, two Americans invited me to a party. It was being given by a prominent town official, they said. An exclusive affair. On no account should I mention it to anyone.

Getting in was a complicated business. One might have been entering a speakeasy. After much whispering through a grille, we were admitted to a small courtyard. Here we were interviewed by a man wearing a llama skin and a *diablada* mask.

"Who is he?" he asked of me.

"He's with us," said the Americans.

I felt enormously privileged when he waved us through. What a letdown, then, when Michele turned up! She'd been passing, she said, and heard a commotion.

She wasn't invited?

She shook her head.

Then how did she get in?

"I told them who I was."

It was a great party, and Michele, to her credit, proved a sensation. She didn't so much dance as scamper, yet it was very fetching, and men fought to take the floor with her. I gained enormously from all of this. Because she and I were assumed to be a couple, those men who wanted to dance with her had first, they thought, to mollify me. This they did by introducing me to their wives and girlfriends. I had a wonderful time, even summoning the courage to kiss several of them.

Even Héctor made an appearance—Héctor whom I had last seen examining his Sisley in La Paz. Too drunk to recognize me, he was upset about something, even threatening to throw himself in front of the first passing car. No one took the threat too seriously. Copacabana's cars had been garaged hours ago.

Carnival had produced in Copacabana a kind of dementia. Even levelheaded Brad succumbed to it, talking the next morning of staying in Bolivia to determine what had happened to Percy Fawcett. Fawcett went missing in Brazil in 1925, and although his body has never been found, he is believed to have perished at the hands of Indians. "I'm convinced he didn't die in Brazil," said Brad. "It's my hunch that he doubled back into Bolivia. Brazil was just a ruse. He was covering his tracks."

Fawcett helped Arthur Conan Doyle write *The Lost World*, and it was just such a place he was seeking when he disappeared. "It is certain," he wrote in 1924, "that amazing ruins of ancient cities—ruins incomparably older than those in Egypt—exist in the far interior of Mato Grosso."

On April 20, 1925, he set off from Cuiabá, reaching Dead Horse Camp six weeks later. It was from here he sent his last dispatch. He was never heard from again. According to Brazilian officials, a search of the area yielded no trace of him.

It was Brad's contention that Fawcett died in the Beni. "That's where his ancient city was," he said. "Look at this." He pulled from his pocket a history of colonial Mojos.

"The Jesuits knew about this place. One of them even said

he saw it. Listen: I'll read you his description—'Its buildings are all of white stone, and it has avenues, plazas, and temples. From the center of a lagoon, the palace of the emperor of Mojos rises, superior to all other structures in size, beauty, and wealth, its doors chained in gold.'

"You know what this place is, don't you? El Dorado! El Dorado's near one of those Jesuit missions. Find it, and I'll bet you anything, you've found Fawcett too."

Bolivians speak fondly of Fawcett. He helped delimit the country's borders, work for which the Royal Geographic Society awarded him its founder's medal in 1917. *Lost Trails, Lost Cities*, his account of his time in Bolivia, is fun to read. I particularly like his tall tales.

In Santa Ana, he claimed, there was "a breed of dog known as the double-nosed Andean tiger hound. The two noses are as clearly divided as though cut by a knife." The animal, he said, was highly regarded for its acute sense of smell.

In Riberalta, he said, there existed a disease whose victims were driven to eat earth. "Possibly the underlying cause was an intestinal parasite. Earth may have served to deaden the irritation. At any rate, a swelling of the body and subsequent death was the result. The Indians knew of only one remedy—dog's excrement—but I never heard of anyone recovering."

The next day, with Carnival winding down, we ascended the hill overlooking Copacabana. Known as Calvary, this is a place of pilgrimage. The stations of the cross mark the route to the top. In front of each is a heap of pebbles. The pebbles represent sin cast off. Journeying upward, it is the custom to augment these heaps with pebbles of one's own. This way, one has attained a state of grace by the time one makes the summit.

Booths along the route sold play money, toy houses, and miniature trucks. There were also tiny replicas of food items: tins of condensed milk and tubes of toothpaste. Purchase these tokens and the objects they represented would be yours within the year.

I had my fortune told by a canary. After its owner held the bird to my face, it picked a card from a drawer. "You have been neglecting your personal affairs," said the card. "But don't worry. Very soon now all your hard work will pay off."

At the top of Calvary were the now-familiar candles and a huge crucifix. The atmosphere reminded one of a rowdy office picnic. Indian women in their best shawls posed with their children for photographs. On the beach below us, a priest was blessing a row of cars and trucks, sprinkling them with water, then raising a hand in benediction.

Several dozen Indians had gathered at the base of the crucifix and were looking across the lake. It was now late afternoon, and they were waiting for the sun to set.

"How long have you been in Bolivia?" a man asked me. He looked familiar. Perhaps I'd met him at the party.

"Three months," I said.

"Well, now you know what it's like to live in the nineteenth century."

He was right. Bolivia *did* exist in the nineteenth century. The value system inherited from Spain in 1825 endures almost intact. The continuity is astonishing. Bolivia today is much as it was when it became a republic. It is a country frozen in the past.

To emancipate itself, to fashion a new society, it needed more than political independence. It had to throw off the Spanish imperial spirit, a task never really attempted. A century and a half after Spain's departure, Bolivia has still to follow the advice of Hegel and cut its ties with Europe. Until it does, it will always be premodern.

The sun was just a few feet above the horizon now, and the crowd on Calvary had grown quiet. All eyes were on the setting sun. It sank lower and lower, slowly easing itself into the lake. And then the sky suddenly filled with clouds, and the sun disappeared from view. All that waiting for nothing. The crowd stood watching a little longer. Perhaps the clouds would clear. But they didn't, and, still silent, the Indians began to pick their way downhill in the thickening dark.

Epilogue

Two days later in La Paz, I ran across Bernardo. He was where he had been when I met him first: leaning against a government car in Plaza Murillo. The circumstances were also similar: another envoy was presenting his credentials to Bolivia's head of state.

"They come and they go," said Bernardo, looking more woebegone than ever. His expression was more careworn than I remembered it, his back more stooped. And he had lost a quantity of hair. I wondered if he were ill. "Soon you'll be going, too, I suppose."

"I leave tomorrow."

"And why not?" he said, summoning a weak smile. "No one stays in Bolivia very long. Unless they have to."

He offered to drive me to the airport.

"But you'll be working," I said.

"I'll take the afternoon off. See you at six."

Bernardo arrived at seven—thirty minutes before my plane was due to leave.

"There's no hurry," he said, easing his car into a traffic jam. "International flights always leave late."

Luckily, mine was not to be the exception. It departed, finally, at 9:45.

"So," he said, as we inched our way up Reforma. "How did you enjoy Bolivia?"

"Very much," I said. In one way or another, I had been asked this question many times before. This was my stock reply. And for a time it was true. I *had* enjoyed Bolivia very much. But that time suddenly seemed long ago. Although I had failed to notice it until just this moment, I had stopped enjoying Bolivia. For nearly a month it had been making me uncomfortable. I was glad to be going home.

"Do you remember a remark you made when we met that first time?" asked Bernardo. "Something about stormy freedom?"

"I said how much I liked it. And you said I'd have had my fill by the time I left."

"And have you?" He looked even more melancholy than he had a day earlier. I had no wish to hurt him.

"You can't have too much freedom," I said.

He looked relieved, although he needn't have. Because you *can* have too much freedom, I knew now. That was the lesson of this trip. An excess of freedom could be just as insupportable as none at all.

I had come to this country certain I'd like it. It was rebellious and unruly and defiant of authority. Rather stupidly, I thought I was too. How could we fail to get along? But Bolivia proved too rich for my blood. It had taught me that I place a greater value on the consolations of society than I realized. Asked, three months ago, which I prized more, impetuosity or restraint, I would have picked the former. But not now. In me the law of measure had its newest champion.

"I've discovered that I'm more like my father than I thought," I told Bernardo.

"Is he a good man?"

"Very good."

"Then you've nothing to worry about."

"The virtuous man," my father was fond of saying, "is one who doesn't make a fuss." I felt a sudden rush of love for him. His tact and his modesty made him worth a dozen Héctors.

Héctor with his European pretensions and his questionable taste. Bolivia was full of Héctors—mining Héctors and drug Héctors, army Héctors and student Héctors—and not one of them was any use to anyone. Acting for themselves alone they created only mischief. Given the freedom to do much as they pleased, they had succeeded only in securing a general discontent. They were proof that when a group insists on exercising its freedoms to their fullest, there is, ultimately, no freedom for anyone. Only insecurity and clamor.

Poor Bolivia. It has almost exhausted its possibilities. Who will save it? Certainly not Héctor. Capacity and power rarely occur in the same person. But there are degrees of incapacity. And Héctor seemed prodigiously inept.

Héctor and his ilk acknowledged no constituency larger than themselves. How could they? Their feelings commanded all their loyalty. Those damn feelings! For all the claims made for them, I should hate to be at their mercy. What Héctor needed was less feeling and more discretion. He needed a sense of decorum—that same decorum Rousseau denounced as tyranny, not realizing that tyranny is decorum's absence.

It will take a lot of decorum to save Bolivia. Decorum will be needed to achieve a more judicious balance between personal liberty and the common good. It will be needed to foster that sense of community without which a country can't survive. Because, first and foremost, Bolivians must want to live together—and right now many of them don't. Where there is no unanimity of mind, said the Italian revolutionary Giuseppe Mazzini, the nation does not exist, "there is only a multitude, a fortuitous agglomeration that any crisis can dissolve."

In place of a nation, there exists in Bolivia an atmosphere of mutual suspicion. Neither the instinct to impose one's will nor the tradition of insubordination that is its by-product is conducive to trust. And trust is what Bolivia needs. Without it, life there will always be more unpredictable, more perilous than it has to be. Without trust, society can confer few benefits.

We were on the Altiplano now, and I could see the airport in the distance. Bernardo took a hand off the steering wheel and blew on it. The evening had turned cold.

"I hate this climate," he said. "I should move to Sucre. Sucre's warm. Did you ever get there?"

"I was just about everywhere: Sucre, Cochabamba, Santa Cruz, Tarija—"

"There was something in the paper about Tarija just this morning. What was it?"

"The strike, maybe?"

"Right. The government sent a man down, didn't it? He's just back."

"Did Tarija get its power plant?"

"It's too soon to say. A report must be written. That could take six months. A year, even."

"I hope Tarija can wait. Passions were running high down there. They may call another strike."

"I doubt that," said Bernardo. "They know the government hasn't any money. All they wanted was attention. I'd say Tarija came out of this rather well."

"You mean this was just another bogus crisis?"

Bernardo winked. "You're getting the picture," he said.

ABOUT THE AUTHOR

A journalist, Eric Lawlor grew up in Ireland and has worked on newspapers there and in England as well as in Canada and the United States. He now lives in New York, where he is completing a novel.